# American Civil War Heroes

*Forgotten Legends and Untold Stories of
Bravery, Sacrifice, and Resilience*

# Table of Contents

# Introduction

Step into the corridors of history with *"American Civil War Heroes,"* a meticulously crafted journey that transcends time and beckons you to discover the untold stories of those who shaped a nation. As you embark on this riveting exploration, prepare to be captivated by a narrative beyond the chronicles of battles and dates, offering a unique and immersive experience tailored for enthusiasts and novices alike.

In the saturated landscape of historical accounts, *"American Civil War Heroes"* distinguishes itself as a beacon of clarity and accessibility. Unlike dense tomes that intimidate the reader with jargon and complexity, this book unfolds seamlessly, inviting readers of all backgrounds to delve into the compelling narrative. Whether you're a seasoned history buff or a newcomer to the subject, the engaging prose and vivid storytelling ensure an enjoyable and enlightening reading experience.

What sets this book apart is its commitment to hands-on exploration of the human experience during the Civil War. It goes beyond the surface, delving into the hearts and minds of the heroes who walked the battlefields. Instead of a dry recitation of facts, it's an invitation to witness the indomitable spirit of those who faced adversity with unwavering courage.

For beginners eager to grasp the intricacies of this pivotal period in American history, *"American Civil War Heroes"* is the perfect introduction. The narrative unfolds with a clarity that demystifies complex events, making it an invaluable resource for those taking their first steps into the fascinating world of Civil War studies. The book acts as a rich guide, leading you through the labyrinth of events without overwhelming you with unnecessary details.

As you turn the pages, you'll find that this isn't just a recounting of historical events but a collection of gripping stories that resonate with the human experience. The heroes of the Civil War come to life through vivid descriptions, allowing you to connect with the individuals who stood at the epicenter of history. It's an immersive journey that transcends time.

In a market flooded with dry accounts and academic treatises, *"American Civil War Heroes"* stands out for its engaging narrative and commitment to making history accessible. The book is a testament to the power of storytelling, ensuring that the remarkable tales within its pages leave an indelible mark on your understanding of the Civil War.

This book is a must-read for those seeking a comprehensive yet easily digestible exploration of the American Civil War. It seamlessly blends historical accuracy with a captivating narrative, offering a gateway to the past that is both educational and enthralling. It's an opportunity to journey through time and witness the extraordinary feats of those who became heroes in the crucible of war. Dive into this compelling narrative and discover a world where courage knew no bounds and the echoes of heroism still resonate today.

# Chapter 1: Elijah P. Marrs: From Slave to Soldier

In the heart of Antebellum Kentucky, where the echoes of slavery reverberated through the tobacco fields and sprawling plantations, a remarkable journey unfolded: a journey that would shape the destiny of Elijah P. Marrs. Born into the cruel shackles of enslavement, his early years were marked by hardship and adversity. This chapter peels back the layers of time to reveal the extraordinary odyssey of Elijah P. Marrs, from his humble beginnings as a slave to his emergence as a courageous soldier in the Union Army.

Rev. E. P. Marrs, D.D.
First Principal of Normal and Theological Institute.

**Elijah P. Marrs emerged as a courageous soldier in the Union Army.**
*https://commons.wikimedia.org/wiki/File:E_P_Marrs.jpg*

To breathe life into Marrs' narrative, direct quotations from his autobiography, "Life and History of the Rev. Elijah P. Marrs," are interwoven throughout the chapter. These poignant excerpts provide a firsthand perspective on his experiences, adding depth and authenticity to recounting his remarkable journey.

# Unveiling the Roots: Elijah P. Marrs' Enslavement and Early Years

The name Elijah P. Marrs symbolizes resilience and triumph against the odds. Born on a Kentucky plantation in 1840, Marrs' journey from enslavement to liberation is a testament to the indomitable spirit that thrives even in the harshest of conditions. It's time to uncover the early life of Elijah P. Marrs, shedding light on the crucible of slavery and the seeds of courage that would sprout into a remarkable legacy.

### The Harsh Reality of Enslavement

Elijah P. Marrs' entry into the world was a testament to the cruel realities faced by enslaved individuals on Kentucky plantations. His autobiography reflects on the shattered familial bonds caused by the oppressive nature of ownership, stating, "*In those days, families were often separated, sold to different masters, and the cry of parting was a familiar sound on every plantation.*" This poignant observation encapsulates the heart-wrenching impact of slavery on family structures, where the whims of owners tore apart the very fabric of kinship.

### Childhood in Bondage

Raised under the oppressive gaze of slavery, Marrs' childhood stood in stark contrast to the warmth of family ties. The relentless rhythm of labor in the fields became the backdrop of his formative years, a poignant reminder of the challenges faced by a slave child. Marrs himself remarked, "*I was a slave, and as such, my early years were filled with toil and hardship.*" His words showcase the harsh reality of a childhood robbed of innocence, where the burdens of labor overshadowed the joys of youth.

### Navigating Challenges

The plantation's fields became a testing ground for Marrs' strength as he navigated the unique challenges of being a slave child. In his own words, "*I knew what it was to be a child slave, and to be a child slave was worse than being an adult slave.*" Marrs' reflection unveils the distinctive hardships faced by young, enslaved individuals grappling with physical demands and the emotional toll of premature responsibilities.

### Resilience Amid Desolation

Despite the oppressive conditions, Marrs' spirit refused to be extinguished. In his autobiography, he noted, *"I felt within me a determination to be free, to enjoy life as other people did."* This inner resolve became the driving force propelling him forward, a flame of resilience that flickered even in the darkest corners of his enslavement. His ability to maintain a sense of self amidst the dehumanizing conditions speaks to the strength of character that would define his future endeavors.

Elijah P. Marrs' early life was more than a tale of hardship. It was a narrative of triumph over adversity. Slavery forged a man whose resilience and courage would echo through history. Through Marrs' words, you glimpse the authentic, firsthand perspective of a soul determined to break free. His journey is a powerful reminder that even in the bleakest circumstances, the human spirit defies oppression and reaches for the light of freedom.

# Breaking Chains: Elijah P. Marrs' Daring Escape to Freedom

In the turbulent pages of American history, certain stories resonate as timeless sagas of resilience, and Elijah P. Marrs' odyssey from enslavement to liberation stands as one of the most remarkable ones. As the nation grappled with the seismic shifts of the Civil War, Marrs sensed an opportunity for change. The winds of transformation whispered through the land, carrying with them the promise of a different tomorrow. The desire for freedom burgeoned within him, intertwining with the zeitgeist of an era marked by upheaval and possibility.

### The Whispers of Change

Marrs' awakening coincided with a nation in flux. The tumultuous climate of the Civil War created ripples of change that even the enslaved could feel. It was a time when hope began to sprout from the soil of despair, and Marrs, attuned to the whispers of change, started envisioning a life unshackled.

### The Burning Desire for Freedom

His decision to escape wasn't a mere reaction to external circumstances. It was a profound manifestation of his inner yearning for liberty. Marrs' spirit burned with an insatiable desire for freedom, a flame that could not be extinguished by the chains that bound his body. The spark within him had illuminated a path toward a future where the shackles of bondage would be replaced by the sweet taste of freedom.

### Navigating Treacherous Paths

The road to freedom was fraught with peril, requiring Marrs to employ cunning and resilience. His escape wasn't a straightforward journey but a complex dance through the shadows, evading those who sought to confine him to a life of bondage. Through the dense forests and moonlit nights, Marrs forged a path to liberty, leaving behind the oppressive yoke that sought to stifle his dreams.

### A Profound Assertion of Humanity

Beyond the physical act of breaking free, Marrs' escape was a profound assertion of his humanity. His autobiography echoes this sentiment, *"To escape was not only to break free from physical chains but to reclaim my humanity."* It was a declaration that he, too, deserved the fundamental rights bestowed upon every human being. Marrs, in his escape, proclaimed that no chains could shackle the inherent dignity of a person.

### The Unyielding Pursuit of Liberty

Marrs' journey transcended the mere act of escaping. It became a relentless pursuit of liberty. Each step resonated with a fervent cry for freedom. His escape transformed into hope for others, yearning for the sweet taste of liberation. In his unyielding pursuit, Marrs became a liberator of himself and a symbol of defiance against the chains of oppression that sought to bind an entire community.

His escape to freedom is a testament to the resilience of the human spirit in the face of oppression. Fueled by an unwavering desire for liberty, his daring journey became a powerful narrative of defiance and triumph. As the shadows of the past gave way to the light of freedom, Marrs' escape shone as a guiding beacon, illuminating the path toward a brighter, more just future. In the darkness of history, his story is proof of the enduring power of the human spirit to rise above adversity and claim the unassailable right to freedom.

# Answering the Call: Elijah P. Marrs and the Union Army Beckons

During the Civil War, enslaved individuals like Elijah P. Marrs found an unprecedented opportunity. It was their chance to transform from chattel to soldiers. It was a pivotal chapter in Marrs' life when the call of the Union Army beckoned, offering him a path from forced labor to the disciplined ranks of the 12th Regiment Heavy Artillery U.S. Colored Troops.

## The Crucible of War and Transformation

The outbreak of the Civil War stirred the air with uncertainty, but for Marrs and countless others, it also carried the promise of liberation. The war became an opportunity for those in bondage to redefine their destinies. Undeterred by the risks looming ahead, Marrs saw a chance for emancipation in this chaos.

## Seizing the Opportunity

In the face of adversity, Marrs seized the chance to enlist in the 12th Regiment Heavy Artillery U.S. Colored Troops. This decision marked a bold declaration of his agency and his refusal to remain confined within the chains of slavery. His enlistment was a manifestation of the courage that stirred within him, echoing the sentiment expressed in his autobiography, *"I seized the opportunity to escape the bondage of chains and embrace the cause of freedom."*

## From Chattel to Soldier

The transition from chattel to soldier was profound, symbolizing a seismic shift in Marrs' identity. No longer relegated to the fields and subjected to the whims of an owner, he stepped into the disciplined ranks of the Union Army, a soldier in the making. His journey mirrored the broader societal transformation occurring as enslaved individuals were given the chance to prove their mettle on the battlefield.

## The 12th Regiment Heavy Artillery U.S. Colored Troops

Enlisting in the 12th Regiment Heavy Artillery, U.S. Colored Troops was more than a military assignment for Marrs. It was a commitment to a cause larger than himself. The regiment, composed of Black soldiers, became a symbol of the Union's recognition of the valor and capability of African-American troops. Marrs, along with his comrades, became a part of a legacy that challenged stereotypes and contributed significantly to the Union war effort.

### Challenges on the Front Lines

Marrs' journey in the Union Army was not without its challenges. The front lines of the Civil War were rife with peril, and the 12th Regiment faced its share of trials. In Marrs' own words, *"The battles were fierce, and the challenges immense, but every hardship we faced on the front lines was a step closer to proving our worth, not just as soldiers but as free men fighting for a better future."*

### A Symbol of Emancipation

Marrs' presence in the Union Army transcended his individual story. It became a symbol of emancipation. His journey from bondage to the battlefield stood out as living proof of the transformative power of the war, challenging the deeply ingrained prejudices of that time. As he fought alongside his fellow soldiers, he wasn't merely defending the Union. He was also fighting for the freedom he had been denied for so long.

### A Pivotal Moment in History

The enlistment of individuals like Elijah P. Marrs in the Union Army marked a pivotal moment in American history. It was a turning point that influenced the outcome of the war and set the stage for the post-war struggles for civil rights. The courage displayed by these soldiers laid the groundwork for a more inclusive vision of the nation where freedom and equality could not be denied based on the color of one's skin.

Elijah P. Marrs' decision to answer the call of the Union Army was a profound act of defiance and hope. When he became a soldier, Marrs contributed to a chapter in history where the shackles of slavery began to unravel. His journey, service, and resilience on the Civil War front lines inspired those who would follow. In the face of war's chaos, Marrs found the opportunity for emancipation and the chance to shape the destiny of a nation undergoing a profound transformation.

# Echoes of Valor: Elijah P. Marrs and Battleground Bravery

In the tumultuous theater of the Civil War, where conflict swept the South, Elijah P. Marrs stood as a paragon of battlefield bravery. His acts of exceptional courage defined his journey. From the relentless barrage of enemy fire to moments of leadership in the chaos of conflict, Marrs endured it all and emerged as a symbol of resilience and tenacity.

### The Essence of Marrs' Battleground Bravery

Marrs' stint as a soldier transcended the conventional expectations of military service. It became a tapestry woven with threads of extraordinary bravery, each strand contributing to the vivid portrait of a man who faced adversity with unwavering determination. His acts of valor became a testament to personal courage and an inspiration to those who fought alongside him.

### The Theater of War

The Southern theater of the Civil War set the stage for Marrs' moments of extraordinary bravery. From the dense forests to the open fields, he confronted the harsh realities of battle, showcasing a resilience forged in the crucible of his early life. Marrs, once confined by chains, now stood tall on the battleground, embodying the spirit of freedom with every step.

### The Battle of Saltville: A Crucible of Valor

One notable chapter in Marrs' journey unfolded during the Battle of Saltville, a pivotal engagement where the 12th Regiment faced formidable Confederate forces. It was here that Marrs' courage reached its zenith, leaving an eternal mark on the regiment's history.

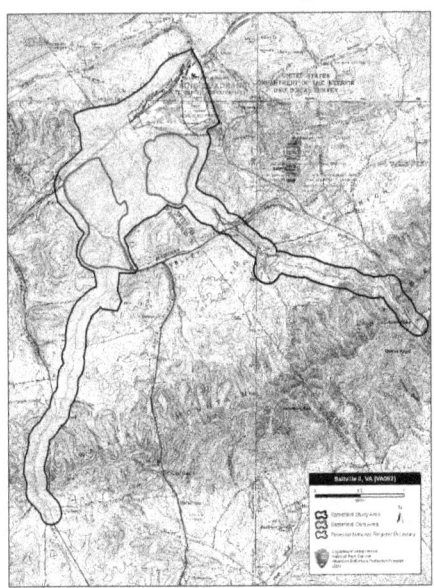

Map of the Battle of Saltville.
*https://commons.wikimedia.org/wiki/File:Saltville_II_Battlefield_Virginia.jpg*

- **Facing Formidable Foes**: As Confederate forces loomed large on the horizon, Marrs and his comrades in the 12th Regiment found themselves in the thick of it all. The enemy's ranks were a formidable force, but Marrs' unwavering commitment to the cause transformed the battleground into a stage for acts of extraordinary bravery.
- **Marrs' Unyielding Commitment**: In the chaos of battle, Marrs' commitment to the Union cause burned brightly. His autobiography provides insights into this moment, *"The Battle of Saltville was more than a clash of armies. It was a clash of ideals. My commitment to the cause surged within me, and I knew that every step on that battlefield was a step toward freedom."*
- **Leadership Amid Adversity**: Amidst the smoke and clamor of battle, Marrs emerged as a leader. His ability to inspire and lead his fellow soldiers through conflict showcased his courage and leadership capacity. Marrs' autobiography captures this sentiment, *"In the face of adversity, leadership was not a choice but a responsibility I embraced for the men who fought beside me."*

In the Civil War, Elijah P. Marrs turned the battleground into a canvas where acts of valor painted a vivid picture of resilience and commitment. From the Battle of Saltville to skirmishes across the South, his journey was defined by more than military service. It was a saga of extraordinary bravery that continues to inspire generations. As you reflect on his battleground bravery, you find a reflection of the indomitable spirit that defined an era of conflict and change.

# Beyond the Battlefield: Education and Ministry

Tales of history often resonate far beyond those of the battlefield, and Elijah P. Marrs' post-war contributions highlight the enduring impact of a life dedicated to service. Freed from the shackles of slavery and military service, Marrs redirected his energy toward education and ministry, becoming a beacon of inspiration for a community yearning for enlightenment.

### A Shift Towards Education

For Elijah P. Marrs, the end of the Civil War signaled a cessation of hostilities and an opening of new avenues. Freed from the oppressive bonds of slavery and the rigors of military service, Marrs recognized the transformative power of education. Denied the pursuit of knowledge in his youth, Marrs turned this longing into a passion for educating others.

### The Transformative Power of Learning

Marrs became a passionate educator, firmly believing in the transformative power of learning. His autobiography reveals, "*Education was the key that unlocked the doors of my emancipation. I wanted others to experience that same liberation through knowledge.*" In the aftermath of war, he tirelessly worked to provide learning opportunities, becoming a guiding light for those who, like him, had been denied access to education.

### Shepherding Souls

Marrs' post-war life also saw him don the mantle of a pastor. The trials and triumphs of war had not only shaped him as a soldier but had forged a man whose commitment to service extended far beyond the battlefield. As a pastor, Marrs shepherded his community toward spiritual enlightenment, providing solace and guidance to those who sought meaning in the aftermath of conflict.

### A Commitment Beyond Boundaries

His commitment extended beyond the walls of his church or the confines of the classroom. His post-war contributions were characterized by an unwavering dedication to service, spreading the values instilled in him during the tumultuous years of the Civil War. In the words of his contemporaries, "*Marrs was not just a soldier. He was a pillar of strength for our community, a beacon of hope for those navigating the complexities of a post-war world.*"

### Legacy of Service

Elijah P. Marrs' post-war legacy is not just a footnote in history. It's a resounding reminder of the enduring impact one individual can have on a community and beyond. His commitment to education and ministry became the guiding light in the aftermath of darkness, a symbol of resilience that transcended the scars of war. His legacy lives on in the pages of history and the lives touched by his dedication to service.

## Legacy Unveiled

The end of the Civil War marked the beginning of a new chapter in Elijah P. Marrs' life. It was a chapter defined not by the battles he fought but by the impact he made beyond the battlefield. His foray into education and ministry became a legacy that continues to inspire. Elijah P. Marrs, the educator and pastor, is an example of the transformative power of learning and the enduring strength of the human spirit. In his post-war pursuits, he became a symbol of enlightenment, proving that the pursuit of knowledge and the service to one's community are endeavors that transcend the boundaries of time and circumstance.

Elijah P. Marrs' life, encapsulated in this chapter, transcends the boundaries of time. His journey from enslavement to the ranks of the Union Army paints a vivid portrait of resilience, courage, and the pursuit of justice. Beyond the battlefield, Marrs' contributions to education and ministry defy the constraints imposed by society.

As you turn to the pages of history, be inspired by Elijah P. Marrs. Watch his legacy echo through the corridors of time. This chapter is an ode to a man whose life epitomized the undying spirit of those who fought for their freedom and the promise of a more just and equitable future.

# Chapter 2: Sarah Emma Edmonds: The Woman Who Fought as a Man

One of the most remarkable Civil War stories was that of a woman named Sarah Emma Edmonds, whose indomitable spirit led her to defy societal norms and become "Frank Thompson" in service to the Union Army. This chapter explores the extraordinary life of Edmonds, from her early years in Canada to her daring exploits as a soldier, nurse, and spy during the Civil War.

Sarah Emma Edmonds defied societal norms to serve in the Union Army.
*https://commons.wikimedia.org/wiki/File:Nurse_and_spy_in_the_Union_Army_-Frontispiece.png*

# Origins of Courage: Early Life in Canada

In the quiet corners of New Brunswick, Canada, a spark of courage was igniting in the formative years of Sarah Emma Edmonds. Born in December 1841, her early life in Canada became the loom on which the threads of defiance and independence were carefully stitched. It's time to uncover the origins of courage that shaped young Sarah's character, from her upbringing in a society steeped in gender expectations to the audacious decision to escape to the United States at age 15.

## The Canadian Tapestry

Born into a world where societal norms dictated strict gender expectations, Sarah Emma Edmonds' childhood unfolded against the backdrop of a society that prescribed narrow roles for men and women. Her strict Canadian upbringing set the stage for the remarkable journey that lay ahead.

In the Edmonds household, young Sarah was confronted with the rigid expectations that governed the roles of women at that time. The societal traditions sought to confine her within predetermined boundaries. However, even in these early years, she displayed a resilience that hinted at the courage she was yet to unveil.

## Escaping Boundaries: Motivations for Emigration

The decision to escape to the United States at the tender age of 15 marked a defining moment in Sarah's life. Motivated by a thirst for independence and a desire for a life unencumbered by societal constraints, her journey across borders became the first bold stroke on the canvas of her extraordinary life.

- **Thirst for Independence:** The allure of independence beckoned to Sarah, transcending the provincial confines of her upbringing. Her autobiography reflects on this pivotal moment, *"The call of independence echoed in my heart, drowning out the societal expectations that sought to confine me. At 15, I chose to follow the path of my own making."*
- **Setting the Stage for Audacious Chapters:** Sarah's emigration to the United States wasn't just a physical relocation. It was the opening act for the audacious chapters that would unfold in her life. The decision to escape served as a declaration of autonomy, a courageous response to the limitations imposed by societal expectations.

# Embracing the Unknown: Life in the United States

Arriving on American soil, Sarah Emma Edmonds stepped into the vast unknown. Her courage, honed in the strict Canadian societal norms, now faced new challenges and opportunities. In the land of the free, she found both the promise of liberty and the complexities of navigating a society undergoing transformation.

- **Forging Identity in a New Land:** The United States became the canvas on which Sarah forged her identity. Freed from the constraints of her upbringing, she embraced the opportunities that a new land offered. Her resilience, shaped by the early challenges in Canada, now intersected with the evolving narrative of American society.
- **A Woman in a Changing America:** As the United States grappled with the winds of change, so did Sarah. Her experiences as a woman in a transforming country added new dimensions to her courage. It was in this dynamic landscape that she would go on to carve her place in history.

Sarah Emma Edmonds' early life in Canada was the catalyst for the courage that would define her remarkable journey. From the confines of gender expectations she was subjected to in her childhood to the audacious decision to break free and immigrate to the United States, each chapter unfolded against a backdrop of defiance and independence.

As you trace the origins of her courage, you'll find a young woman who dared to dream of a life beyond boundaries – despite societal norms. Little did she know that this courage, cultivated in the quiet corners of New Brunswick, would propel her into the annals of history as a figure of resilience, independence, and trailblazing bravery.

# Enlistment and Transformation: Becoming Frank Thompson

Amidst the chaos of the Civil War, Sarah Edmonds made a courageous decision that transcended societal norms and gender expectations. She enlisted in the Union Army. But this was not a mere enlistment. It was a profound transformation. Adopting the persona of "Frank Thompson," she navigated the complexities of war, reshaping her destiny in unimaginable ways. Sarah's enlistment was pivotal as she explored the 2nd Michigan Infantry and the multifaceted role she assumed as a combatant, nurse, and later a spy.

# Choosing Liberty over Convention: Enlisting in the Union Army

The year 1861 bore witness to the nation being engulfed in the flames of the Civil War. It was during this tumultuous period that Sarah Edmonds, driven by a fervent desire for liberty and freedom from traditional female roles, made a bold choice that would forever alter her destiny.

- **A Bold Decision:** Enlisting in the Union Army was more than a response to the call of duty; it was a declaration of autonomy. Fearing the suffocating constraints of societal expectations for women, Sarah embraced the guise of "Frank Thompson," a persona that would become the key to her transformation.
- **Embracing a New Identity:** "Frank Thompson" became a shield that allowed Sarah to navigate a world dominated by men. Her enlistment was an opportunity to redefine her identity on her own terms.

### The 2nd Michigan Infantry: A New Identity

Within the ranks of the 2nd Michigan Infantry, Sarah's metamorphosis into Frank Thompson reached completion. The regiment became where her multifaceted roles would evolve.

- **Rigorous Training and Camaraderie:** As a soldier within the 2nd Michigan Infantry, Sarah underwent rigorous training, honing the skills necessary for survival on the front lines. The camaraderie with fellow troops provided a sense of belonging, even as she concealed her true identity beneath the uniform of "Frank Thompson."
- **A Multifaceted Role Unveiled:** Her time in the 2nd Michigan Infantry marked the unveiling of Sarah's multifaceted role. As a combatant, she faced the harsh realities of war, standing shoulder to shoulder with her comrades. As a nurse, she tended to the wounded, providing comfort amid the chaos. It was during this time that her innate sense of duty and courage became evident.

### A Spy in the Ranks

As Sarah embraced her role within the regiment, another layer of her transformation emerged. She became a spy. Operating behind enemy lines, she gathered crucial intelligence, risking her life for the Union's cause. The pages of history would later reveal her clandestine activities, painting a portrait of courage in the face of danger.

- **Gathering Intelligence:** Sarah's forays as a spy showcased her bravery and strategic acumen. Behind enemy lines, she navigated the complexities of espionage, collecting vital information that would prove instrumental in shaping the course of battles.
- **The Unveiling of True Identity:** The culmination of Sarah's service came with the revelation of her true identity. Despite the risks, she chose to unveil herself and face potential consequences. Her choice to reveal the truth spoke to the authenticity of her commitment and the courage that defined her wartime service.

Sarah Edmonds' enlistment and transformation into Frank Thompson is a testament to the transformative power of courage. She defied societal norms, reshaping her destiny and the perception of what women could achieve. Her journey within the 2nd Michigan Infantry, from combatant to nurse and spy, tells a story of resilience, adaptability, and unwavering commitment. As you reflect on her legacy, you find not only a soldier but also a trailblazer whose courage echoes through the annals of history. She's a woman who chose liberty over convention and, in doing so, transformed her destiny.

# Deeper Dive into Edmonds' Contributions

Sarah Emma Edmonds, a name etched in Civil War history, transcended the confines of conventional roles for women during her multifaceted service in the 2nd Michigan Infantry. Whether as a combatant on the front lines, a compassionate nurse tending to the wounded, or a shadowy figure spying behind enemy lines, her legacy is one of unparalleled courage and commitment.

### On the Front Lines: Combatant in the 2nd Michigan Infantry

Her enlistment in the 2nd Michigan Infantry marked the beginning of a remarkable journey where she shattered gender norms and proved herself to be a capable combatant. In a time when women were largely confined to traditional roles, Sarah's actions on the battlefield became a resounding testament to her dedication to the Union cause.

- **Breaking Gender Barriers**: Sarah's service as a combatant defied the prevalent notions of the time. Despite the limitations imposed on women, she exhibited a level of courage that rivaled her male counterparts. Her commitment to the front lines showcased her determination and unwavering resolve to contribute to the Union's fight for liberty.
- **A Testament to Dedication:** Her actions on the battlefield were not merely symbolic. They were a tangible demonstration of dedication. Sarah's service within the 2nd Michigan Infantry exemplified her commitment to the ideals of freedom and equality, reverberating with each step taken on the grounds of conflict.

### Tending to Wounds and Comforting Souls: A Nurse in the Union Army

Beyond the intensity of battle, Sarah assumed the role of a compassionate nurse, embodying empathy amid the war's brutality. Her dedication to alleviating the suffering of her fellow soldiers illustrated a different facet of her contributions.

- **Compassion Amid Chaos**: As a nurse in the Union Army, Sarah provided solace to those scarred by the physical and emotional ravages of war. Her compassionate care transcended the boundaries of duty, earning her the respect and admiration of her comrades.
- **Building Camaraderie through Care:** Her nursing role not only contributed to the physical well-being of the wounded but also fostered a sense of camaraderie among the troops. Sarah's presence in the medical corps became a source of reassurance, a testament to her ability to nurture the human spirit in the middle of the grim realities of war.

# Veiled in Shadows: The Espionage of Frank Thompson

Yet, perhaps the most extraordinary chapter of Sarah's service unfolded during her time as a spy. Under the guise of Frank Thompson, she undertook daring missions behind enemy lines, transcending the conventional roles expected of women during the era.

- **A Mysterious Operative:** Frank Thompson's covert operations painted Sarah as a mysterious operative, navigating the treacherous landscape of espionage with finesse. Her ability to elude detection and gather crucial intelligence showcased her strategic acumen and fearless resolve to contribute to the Union's triumph.
- **A Legendary Spy:** Her days in espionage would carve her name in history as one of the most effective spies of the Civil War. Her daring missions, undertaken at great personal risk, became legendary and embodied the spirit of sacrifice and dedication to a cause larger than herself.

Sarah Emma Edmonds' trifecta of roles epitomized courage, versatility, and an unyielding commitment to the Union cause. In each capacity, she defied societal norms, leaving a mark on the narrative of the Civil War. As you reflect on her legacy, you find a woman who transcended the limitations of her time and a symbol of solidity whose contributions resonate through the pages of history.

### Daring Espionage Missions: Behind Enemy Lines

In the shadows of the Civil War, where secrets held the power to sway battles, Sarah Emma Edmonds embarked on daring espionage missions. It's time to look at Sarah's silent valor as she infiltrated Confederate territory, gathering intelligence that proved instrumental in shaping Union strategy.

### Infiltrating Confederate Territory

Sarah's espionage missions were not for the faint of heart. Venturing deep into Confederate territory, where danger lurked in every corner, she embraced the challenge with unwavering determination. Disguised as a Confederate soldier, she navigated the precarious terrain of espionage with remarkable finesse.

- **The Stakes and Risks:** The very nature of infiltrating enemy lines elevated the stakes of Sarah's espionage endeavors. Every step she took was shadowed by the constant threat of exposure, capture, and the dire consequences that accompanied such revelations. In the heart of Confederate territory, the risks she faced were as high as the stakes of the war itself.
- **Navigating Precarious Terrain:** In the intricate perils of espionage, Sarah demonstrated a rare ability to navigate the precarious terrain with finesse. Her disguise as a Confederate

soldier wasn't just a costume. It became a shield that allowed her to move unnoticed, extracting vital information that would alter the course of battles.

### Gathering Intelligence: The Value of Risk

Sarah's espionage activities were calculated risks that held immense value for the Union war effort. Her ability to gather intelligence, from troop movements to strategic plans, became a linchpin in shaping Union strategy on the battlefield.

- **Instrumental Reports**: Sarah's reports, derived from her daring forays behind enemy lines, played a pivotal role in providing Union commanders with critical information. The intelligence she gathered became a strategic asset, offering insights that influenced decisions on troop deployments, defensive postures, and counteroffensives.

- **Personal Risks and Strategic Rewards**: The risks Sarah took weren't just personal. They were integral to the broader Union war effort. Each clandestine mission carried the weight of potential discovery and the severe consequences that accompanied it. Yet, her commitment to the cause transcended personal safety, embodying a selfless dedication to the Union's triumph.

### The Toll of Deception: The Weight of Secrets

The life of a spy is one of perpetual deception, and Sarah bore the weight of her secrets with stoic resolve. The toll on her mental and emotional well-being was profound, yet she pressed on, driven by an unwavering commitment to the cause she had adopted as her own.

- **Constant Deception**: The art of espionage demanded a constant facade of deception. Sarah lived a dual existence, balancing her role as a Confederate soldier with her allegiance to the Union cause. The burden of maintaining this facade, day in and day out, became a silent weight on her shoulders.

- **Unwavering Commitment**: Despite the toll, Sarah's commitment to the Union cause remained unwavering. Her endurance in the face of constant deception reflected a profound sense of duty. The sacrifices she made behind enemy lines, both tangible and intangible, became the silent currency of her commitment.

Sarah Emma Edmonds' daring espionage missions behind enemy lines made a mark in the history of the Civil War. In the silent corridors of deception, her contributions became instrumental in shaping the narrative of battles. As you reflect on her silent valor, you'll find a woman whose unwavering commitment and calculated risks contributed greatly to the Union's triumph.

# Post-War Pursuits: From Espionage to Advocacy

As the echoes of the Civil War faded, Sarah Emma Edmonds found herself in a different kind of battle. It was a battle for recognition of her invaluable contributions. Despite facing bureaucratic hurdles and entrenched gender norms, she persisted in seeking acknowledgment for her military service. This section explores Sarah's post-war struggle for a pension and her literary legacy, encapsulated in the groundbreaking memoir, "Nurse and Spy in the Union Army."

### The Battle for a Pension

The war's conclusion marked the beginning of a new struggle for Sarah. Despite her daring exploits as a soldier, nurse, and spy, receiving recognition in the form of a pension proved elusive. Bureaucracy and deeply entrenched gender norms initially thwarted her efforts, but undeterred, she persisted in her pursuit of acknowledgment.

- **Thwarted by Bureaucracy:** The bureaucracy of post-war administration presented formidable obstacles for veterans seeking acknowledgment. Sarah's gender further complicated matters, as the system was ill-prepared to recognize the contributions of a woman who had defied convention to serve her country.
- **Persistence in Pursuit:** Undeterred by the bureaucratic hurdles, Sarah displayed resilience in her pursuit of recognition. Her determination mirrored the same spirit that had led her through the dangers of the battlefield. Despite facing systemic barriers, she pressed forward, refusing to let her contributions be relegated to the shadows.

### A Literary Legacy: "Nurse and Spy in the Union Army"

In 1865, Sarah Emma Edmonds took pen to paper and wrote her memoir, "Nurse and Spy in the Union Army." Published under her pseudonym, Frank Thompson, the groundbreaking account brought her experiences during the war to light, providing a rare firsthand account of the life of a woman who defied convention to serve her country.

- **A Rare Firsthand Perspective**: The memoir was a literary testament to Sarah's multifaceted service. It offered readers a rare glimpse into the life of a woman who had navigated the perils of the battlefield, tended to the wounded as a nurse, and ventured into espionage behind enemy lines. Through her words, she sought to shatter preconceived notions about the roles women could play in times of conflict.
- **Defiance of Convention**: Published under her pseudonym, the memoir became a symbolic act of defiance against societal norms. By choosing to reveal her experiences through the guise of Frank Thompson, Sarah emphasized the importance of the narrative itself, underscoring the challenges she faced as a woman in a male-dominated space.

# Recognition and Beyond the Legacy of Sarah Emma Edmonds

Sarah's persistence in seeking recognition eventually bore fruit when, in 1884, she was granted a pension for her military service. However, her legacy extends far beyond the bureaucratic battles. Through her memoir and the acknowledgment of her contributions, Sarah paved the way for future generations of women who aspired to break free from societal constraints.

- **A Pioneering Legacy**: Sarah Emma Edmonds' legacy is one of pioneering courage and determination. Beyond the battles on the battlefield and bureaucratic hurdles, she became a trailblazer whose literary contributions and quest for recognition opened doors for women in the military and beyond.
- **Inspiring Future Generations**: Through her memoir and the recognition of her service, Sarah inspired future generations of women to challenge societal norms. Her story inspired those who dared to defy convention, showing that courage knows no gender and contributions amid adversity deserve acknowledgment.

The post-war battle for recognition was a victory in itself, but Sarah Emma Edmonds' legacy extends far beyond the pension she eventually received. Through her memoir, she ensured that her experiences, and by extension, the experiences of women in the military, were documented and celebrated. In her literary legacy and the recognition she sought, Sarah Emma Edmonds symbolizes fortitude and the enduring spirit that transcends the challenges of both war and societal norms.

## Legacy and Commemoration

Sarah Emma Edmonds' legacy transcends the pages of history. Her courageous journey challenges traditional narratives. Today, efforts are ongoing to ensure her contributions are recognized and celebrated. The tale of Sarah Emma Edmonds is an enduring testament to the power of courage and resilience. Her life inspires countless individuals to challenge boundaries, demonstrating that one person, driven by conviction, can alter the course of history.

In the annals of the Civil War, the story of Sarah Emma Edmonds reflects the unbending spirit that defies conventions and expectations. From her humble beginnings in Canada to her daring espionage missions behind enemy lines, Edmonds' journey resonates with courage, strength, and unwavering commitment to the ideals of freedom and justice. Her legacy endures, challenging you to reevaluate preconceived notions and embrace the courage within yourself, just as she did on the battlefields of the Civil War.

# Chapter 3: Albert Cashier: The Transgender Soldier

In the corners of the American Civil War, threads of diversity and fortitude utter a narrative that transcends the conventional tales of battles and heroes. Albert Cashier, a transgender soldier who defied societal norms by serving under the guise of male identity, emerges as a poignant figure in this complex tableau. His story unfolds on the battlefields of the Civil War and traverses the uncharted terrain of gender identity in a society grappling with the aftermath of conflict.

Albert Cashier was a transgender soldier who served under the guise of male identity.

# Early Life and Migration: A Journey to Identity

Albert Cashier's journey begins not on the fields of war but in the picturesque landscapes of Ireland. Born as Jennie Irene Hodgers, Cashier's early life in Ireland seems shrouded in the mists of the 19th century. The decision to migrate to the United States marked a pivotal moment, leading to the adoption of a new identity, that of Albert Cashier.

## Adoption of a New Identity

As mentioned, precise details surrounding Albert Cashier's early life in 1840s Ireland remain a bit obscure. However, historians believe he was born Jennie Irene Hodgers and began living as a boy at a young age. Theories about the reasons for this transition vary, with some suggesting a harsh stepfather demanding an extra hand, while others point to a deeper yearning to defy societal norms and embrace a gender identity that felt more authentic.

Whatever the specific motivation, the decision to adopt the male identity of Albert Cashier marked a pivotal moment, setting the stage for an extraordinary journey that would unfold across war-torn battlefields and the uncharted territory of gender identity in a society that was very unaccepting at the time.

In 1862, driven by a restless spirit and seeking new opportunities, Albert Cashier embarked on a journey across the Atlantic to the United States. This emigration marked another pivotal chapter in his life, offering a fresh start and the potential for a future free from the constraints of his past. With its ideals of liberty and equality, the burgeoning American nation held a particular allure for Albert, whose desire for self-determination resonated with the nation's founding principles.

## Enlistment in the 95th Illinois Infantry

Upon reaching American soil, Albert Cashier felt the call to arms as the Civil War raged across the nation. Witnessing the conflict unfold, the ideals of freedom and equality he sought resonated with the cause of the Union. Fueled by a sense of patriotism and a desire to contribute to a greater purpose, Albert boldly decided to enlist in the 95th Illinois Infantry Regiment. This act of service signified his dedication to the Union cause and a continued embrace of the identity he had forged for himself as a man.

However, maintaining this identity within the close-knit community of soldiers presented unique challenges. Albert faced the constant risk of exposure and potential discrimination, adding a layer of complexity to his military service. He navigated these challenges with unwavering courage and a commitment to his duties, earning the respect and admiration of his comrades. Albert Cashier established himself as a valued regiment member through his dedication and bravery, proving that his true worth lay not in his assigned gender at birth but in his character, courage, and unwavering spirit.

### The Dual Identity Dilemma

Albert Cashier's dual existence was not merely logistical. It was a psychological labyrinth he navigated daily. The relentless demands of war and fear of exposure took a toll on him. Living as a man while harboring a secret created internal conflict, likely manifesting as anxiety, depression, and isolation. The ever-present threat of exposure added further strain, leading to hypervigilance and constant anxiety.

Despite these challenges, Albert demonstrated remarkable resilience. He navigated his dual identity with grace and courage, finding solace in his comrades and purpose in serving his country. Examining Albert's dual identity sheds light on the broader societal implications of gender identity and the challenges faced by those who defy traditional expectations. It encourages you to consider the nuanced experiences of those who navigate the world with a hidden truth, paving the way for a more inclusive and accepting society.

# Battleground Bravery: A Soldier's Journey

Albert Cashier's military service unfolded amidst the chaos and turmoil of the Civil War. He participated in several key battles, including the grueling Siege of Vicksburg and the perilous Red River Campaign. Through these experiences, he demonstrated his unwavering resolve and the profound bonds of brotherhood forged in the crucible of war.

### The Siege of Vicksburg

The Siege of Vicksburg was a defining moment in Albert Cashier's life. He endured the relentless bombardment, the daily hardships of camp life, and the constant threat of enemy fire. His courage and resilience shone through during this harrowing ordeal as he steadfastly performed his duties alongside his fellow soldiers. His actions during the siege cemented his reputation as a reliable comrade, earning his fellow soldiers' respect and admiration.

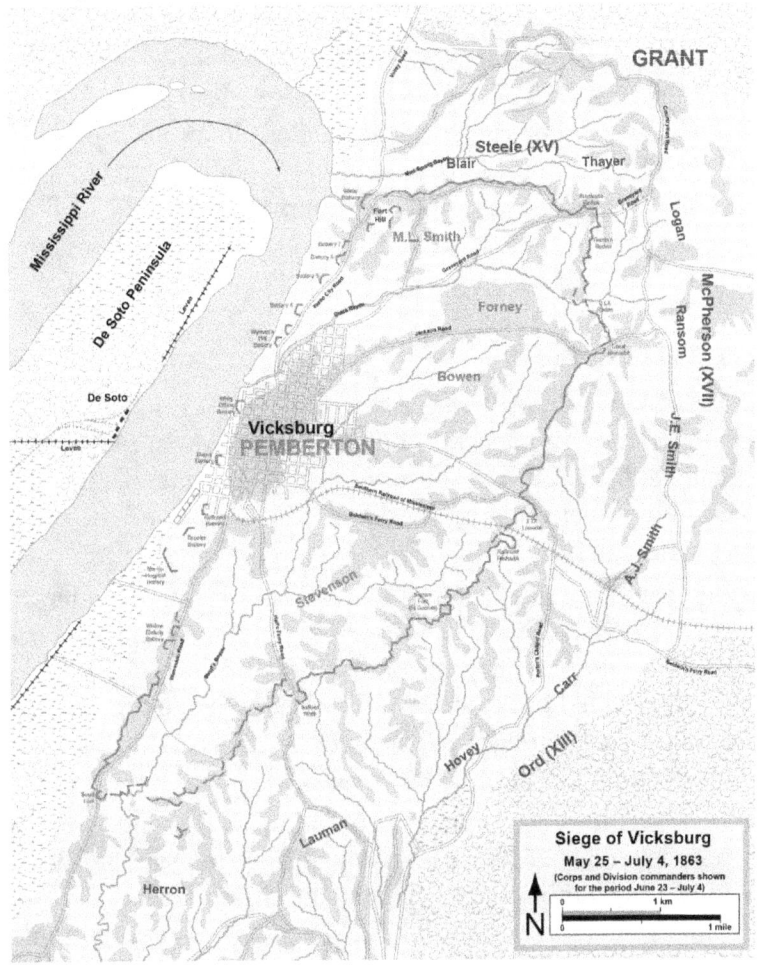

**Map of the Siege of Vicksburg.**
*Map by Hal Jespersen, www.posix.com/CW, CC BY 3.0*
*<https://creativecommons.org/licenses/by/3.0>, via Wikimedia Commons:*
*https://commons.wikimedia.org/wiki/File:VicksburgSiege.png*

Beyond his bravery, Albert also experienced the profound sense of camaraderie that defined the wartime experience. Sharing meals, stories, and laughter with his comrades, he formed bonds that transcended the boundaries of rank and identity. These bonds would serve as a source of strength and support throughout the war and in the following years.

### The Red River Campaign

The Red River Campaign further tested Albert Cashier's mettle. He navigated the treacherous swamps and bayous of the South, facing the enemy and the harsh realities of disease and weather. Through it all, he displayed exceptional strength and unwavering courage. He earned the trust and respect of his superiors, who recognized his leadership qualities and willingness to go the extra mile for his comrades.

Albert Cashier's experiences in the Red River Campaign further solidified his place within the regiment. He emerged as a respected and admired soldier, his courage and dedication inspiring his fellow men. His wartime service demonstrated that personal identity, in all its complexities, does not diminish one's ability to serve with distinction and honor.

### Bonds Forged in Battle

In the chaos of war, Albert Cashier found solace in the unexpected haven of brotherhood forged with his fellow soldiers. In the trenches and on the battlefield, shared hardships and triumphs created a unique bond that transcended societal norms and offered acceptance for someone navigating a dual identity.

Wartime camaraderie shattered barriers and fostered understanding, regardless of individual backgrounds. Soldiers united under a common purpose, finding comfort and support in each other. For Cashier, this brotherhood provided a safe space free from the judgment he might face in civilian life. His courage and stability, witnessed by his comrades, earned him respect and unwavering loyalty.

Firsthand accounts illustrate the depth of this bond. One soldier recalls Cashier's courage inspiring him during the Siege of Vicksburg, while another remembers shared laughter around campfires, offering respite from the horrors of war. These anecdotes paint a vivid picture of their connection, a testament to the unwavering support Cashier received.

Even after the war, these bonds remained strong. When Cashier's dual identity was revealed, his comrades rallied to his defense, writing letters and testifying to his character. Despite potential social disapproval, their unwavering commitment speaks volumes about the depth of their connection and belief in him. Albert Cashier's wartime bonds are proof of the power of human connection. They transcend societal norms and demonstrate that even against adversity, acceptance and support can be found.

# Post-War Challenges: Navigating a Dual Existence

The end of the war did not herald a return to normalcy for Albert Cashier. Instead, it marked the beginning of a different battle. It was a battle for acceptance and understanding in a society grappling with the scars of war. Cashier's life in post-war Illinois becomes a poignant exploration of the challenges faced by a transgender individual in a world that clung to rigid gender norms.

## Living as a Man

Albert Cashier's post-war life was marked by a constant effort to maintain the male identity he had established. He worked various jobs, including farmhand, church janitor, and street lamplighter, integrating himself into the community while carefully concealing his assigned gender at birth. This required constant vigilance and awareness, a mental burden that he carried day in and day out. He knew that even the slightest slip could lead to exposure and potential ostracization.

Despite these challenges, Albert Cashier continued to live his life with dignity and grace. He formed friendships and relationships within the community, earning the respect and trust of those around him. His kindness, humor, and strong work ethic were recognized by all those who encountered him. He became a familiar figure in Saunemin, a respected member of the community who had bravely served his country and now sought to build a peaceful life for himself.

## Discovery of Gender Identity

In 1910, Albert Cashier's carefully constructed life was shattered. A broken leg led to a medical examination that revealed his assigned sex at birth. This revelation sent shockwaves through the community, triggering public scrutiny and accusations of fraud. The pension he had earned through his military service was now threatened, and his livelihood was jeopardized.

The discovery of Albert Cashier's gender identity forced him to confront societal prejudices head-on. He faced public ridicule and condemnation, with some questioning his character and even his right to be recognized as a veteran. This period of his life was undoubtedly one of immense hardship as he grappled with the loss of privacy and the scrutiny he received.

However, Albert Cashier did not succumb to despair. He drew strength from the support of his friends and family, and especially from his fellow Civil War veterans. These men, who had witnessed his courage and resilience on the battlefield, rallied to his defense. They testified to his character, service, and unwavering dedication to his duties. They fought to ensure that he received the pension he rightfully earned, demonstrating the enduring power of the bonds forged in war.

### The Brotherhood of Comrades

Albert Cashier's story highlights the profound impact of wartime bonds. The brotherhood forged on the battlefields of the Civil War transcended societal norms and prejudices, providing Albert with a crucial source of support and understanding during a time of immense difficulty. His comrades, who had shared the hardships and triumphs of war with him, refused to abandon him in his hour of need. Their unwavering support and actions paved the way for a more inclusive and understanding society.

### Support from Civil War Comrades

The support Albert Cashier received from his comrades was remarkable and multifaceted. When his pension was threatened, they organized a campaign to ensure he received the benefits he had earned. They wrote letters, testified before committees, and even collected donations to help him financially. Their tireless efforts were instrumental in securing his pension, a victory that resonated beyond Albert Cashier's case. It highlighted the importance of honoring the sacrifices of all veterans, regardless of their circumstances.

### Broader Implications

The support Albert Cashier received from his comrades also had broader societal implications. It challenged the prevailing notions of masculinity and gender identity in the post-war era. It demonstrated that true courage and resilience extended beyond the battlefield and encompassed the ability to stand up for what is right, even in the face of adversity. Albert Cashier's story became a ray of hope for marginalized communities, inspiring others to fight for their rights and recognition.

# Beyond Albert: Ripple Effects and Unfolding Narratives

While Albert Cashier's story showcases courage and solidity, his journey also serves as a starting point for exploring the broader experiences of transgender veterans. Investigating the impact of his case and subsequent recognition of other veterans sheds light on the evolving landscape of inclusivity and acceptance within the military and veteran communities.

### Opening Avenues for Recognition

Albert's case, while facing initial challenges and scrutiny, paved the way for increased awareness and recognition of transgender veterans. His story sparked conversations about gender identity within the Department of Veterans Affairs and military institutions. It led to a gradual shift in policies and procedures, creating a framework for recognizing and supporting transgender veterans in accessing benefits and services.

One notable example is the 2016 Veterans Affairs Directive 1300.28, which explicitly prohibits discrimination based on gender identity and ensures access to medically necessary care for transgender veterans. This policy change, directly influenced by Cashier's case and the advocacy efforts surrounding it, marked a significant step toward inclusivity within the VA.

### Acknowledging Untold Stories

Albert's case also inspired further research and recognition of other transgender veterans whose stories were previously marginalized or ignored. As awareness of Cashier's story grew, historians and researchers began uncovering the experiences of other transgender individuals who served in the military. It led to the documentation of numerous cases, shedding light on the diverse experiences of transgender individuals across different generations and branches of the military.

One such example is the story of Lucy Ann Lobdell, a transgender woman who disguised herself as a man to enlist in the Union Army during the Civil War. Lobdell's story, similar to Cashier's, was largely unknown until recent research brought it to light. Recognizing these diverse narratives paints a more comprehensive picture of the transgender military experience and highlights the ongoing need for inclusivity and support.

### Ripple Effects on Veteran Communities

The advocacy efforts surrounding Cashier's case impacted policy and recognition but also had a ripple effect on the attitudes and perceptions within veteran communities. Many veterans, inspired by Cashier's story and the fight for his recognition, became vocal advocates for LGBTQ+ rights within their communities. It led to the creation of veteran support groups and organizations dedicated to fostering inclusivity and understanding.

One example is the American Veterans for Equal Rights (AVER), an organization founded by transgender veterans in 1990. AVER works to ensure equal rights and benefits for all veterans, regardless of sexual orientation or gender identity. Their work, directly inspired by Cashier's legacy, demonstrates the ongoing commitment of veterans to fight for inclusivity and equality within their community.

### Unfolding Narratives and Ongoing Challenges

The journey toward full acceptance and recognition for transgender veterans continues. While significant progress has been made in recent years, challenges and inequalities remain. Access to healthcare, housing, and employment is still difficult for transgender veterans, and societal biases and discrimination persist.

Despite these challenges, Cashier's legacy remains a powerful symbol of hope and inspiration for transgender veterans and their allies. His story is a reminder of the importance of fighting for equality and inclusion. It encourages ongoing efforts to create a more just and equitable society where all veterans are valued and respected. As the stories of more transgender veterans come to light and their voices are amplified, the path toward full acceptance and recognition continues to unfold.

# Legacy and Reflections: An Unconventional Life

Albert Cashier's life, both in and out of uniform, portrays the complexities of identity and the enduring power of the human spirit. His story transcends the conventional narratives of the Civil War, inviting you to consider the experiences of those who defied societal norms and fought for the right to be themselves. His legacy inspires you to challenge prejudices, embrace diversity, and strive for a more inclusive world.

### Recognition and Acceptance

While Albert Cashier did not receive widespread recognition for his service during his lifetime, his story has steadily gained attention in recent years. Books, documentaries, and articles have shed light on his experiences, raising awareness of the challenges faced by transgender individuals and the importance of inclusivity. In 2011, the Illinois House of Representatives passed a resolution recognizing Cashier's service and expressing regret for the discrimination he faced. In 2023, the United States Department of Veterans Affairs announced plans to issue Cashier a new headstone with his preferred name and gender marker, a long-awaited act of recognition and respect.

Despite these advancements, much work remains to be done to ensure full acceptance and understanding of transgender identities. Cashier's story is a powerful reminder of the ongoing struggle for equality and justice for all individuals, regardless of gender identity or expression.

### Broader Societal Implications

Beyond individual recognition, Albert Cashier's story has broader societal implications that continue to resonate today. His life challenges traditional understandings of masculinity and gender roles, prompting people to reconsider their assumptions and biases. He demonstrates that courage, bravery, and patriotism exist beyond the boundaries of conventional gender norms.

Furthermore, Cashier's story sheds light on the importance of historical inclusion and the need to acknowledge diverse experiences within narratives of war and conflict. His presence in the Civil War narrative complicates existing understandings of the war and encourages you to consider the experiences of marginalized groups who often remain invisible in history lessons.

### Inspiration for Future Generations

Albert Cashier's life is an enduring source of inspiration for future generations. His courage in spite of the adversity facing him, his unwavering commitment to his identity, and his fight for recognition and respect inspire others to embrace their identities and stand up for their beliefs. His story reminds you that true heroism comes in many forms and that even the most unconventional individuals can leave a lasting impact on the world.

## Unanswered Questions and Ongoing Research

While Albert Cashier's story has been brought to light in recent years, there are still many unanswered questions about his life. Historians continue to research and uncover new details about his early life, his experiences during the war, and his post-war challenges. This ongoing research is crucial to understanding Cashier's experiences and the broader context of transgender history.

## A Call to Action for Change

Albert Cashier's story not only inspires but also compels you to action. It is a call to action for a more inclusive and equitable society where all individuals are valued and respected for who they are. By learning from Cashier's experiences and understanding his challenges, you can work toward creating a world where everyone feels safe to live authentically and contribute their unique talents and perspectives to society. The legacy of Albert Cashier continues to unfold, reminding you of the importance of personal courage, societal inclusion, and the ongoing struggle for justice and equality for all.

## A Transcendent Tale of War and Identity

Albert Cashier's story is not merely a footnote in history but a vibrant tapestry woven with threads of war, identity, and the enduring power of the human spirit. He transcended the confines of societal expectations, defying gender norms and bravely serving his country in a time of great conflict. His legacy extends beyond the battlefield, reminding you that courage takes many forms and that true heroism lies in the unwavering pursuit of authenticity and acceptance.

## Symbol of Courage and Resilience

Albert Cashier's life is a testament to the profound bravery and strength required to live authentically despite societal prejudice. He exemplifies the strength of the human spirit in the face of adversity, and his story inspires all who face discrimination or marginalization. His unwavering commitment to his identity and refusal to be silenced continue to resonate with individuals and communities fighting for their rights and recognition.

## Beyond the Binary

Albert Cashier's story highlights the experiences of those who did not fit neatly into conventional categories. His life compels you to move beyond binary notions of gender and identity, recognizing the spectrum of human experience and the importance of celebrating diversity. Through his life, Albert Cashier invites you to expand your understanding of what it means to be a soldier, a citizen, and a human being.

## A Legacy for the Future

Albert Cashier's legacy lives on in the ongoing struggle for LGBTQ+ rights and the fight for a more inclusive and understanding society. His story is a powerful reminder that progress is possible and that even the smallest acts of courage contribute to a more just and equitable world. By remembering and learning from his life, you'll continue to challenge discrimination, promote acceptance, and ensure everyone can live a life of dignity and respect.

Albert Cashier's journey, from the battlefields of the Civil War to the quiet streets of Saunemin, Illinois, offers a powerful and enduring message about the human spirit's capacity for fearlessness, stability, and the unwavering pursuit of self-determination. He reminds you that true heroism lies not in conforming to societal expectations but in embracing your authentic self and fighting for the right to be recognized and respected. His legacy urges you to strive for a world where diversity is celebrated, and everyone has the freedom to live authentically and proudly.

# Chapter 4: William Harvey Carney: Holding the Flag High

Born into enslavement, William Harvey Carney's journey from Virginia to Massachusetts symbolizes personal liberation and the broader struggle for freedom and equality. Are you ready to explore the monumental achievements of Carney, the first African American to receive the Medal of Honor? This chapter emphasizes his heroic stand as a member of the 54th Massachusetts Infantry Regiment during the assault on Fort Wagner.

William Harvey Carney's journey symbolizes personal liberation.

# From Enslavement to Freedom: The Early Years

William Harvey Carney's life story imparts hope despite overwhelming adversity. Born into the suffocating shackles of slavery in Virginia, he refused to accept his circumstances. His journey from being an enslaved child to a man who dared to dream of freedom is an inspiring testament to the unyielding human spirit.

## Enslaved in Virginia

William's formative years were shrouded in the oppressive reality of plantation life. He was born into a world where his life was not his own, where his every breath was a tribute to the whims of another. The Virginia of his youth was a brutal landscape, a place where families were torn apart. Dreams were crushed under the relentless weight of cruelty.

William, like many enslaved individuals, was denied the necessities of life. He witnessed firsthand the horrors of physical abuse and the emotional toll of endless toil. The plantation became his prison, a place where humanity was stripped away, and survival became the only measure of success.

Despite the suffocating environment, William's spirit refused to be extinguished. He yearned for a life beyond the confines of the plantation, a life where he could choose his path and chase his dreams. He clung to the stories of freedom whispered in the darkness, stories that fueled the embers of hope burning bright within his soul.

## Escape to Massachusetts

In the dead of night, under the cloak of darkness, William took a leap of faith. He embarked on a perilous journey, risking everything for a chance at freedom. He faced numerous dangers, the threat of capture ever-present. Each step forward was fraught with uncertainty, each decision carrying the weight of life and death.

The journey north was a test of William's strength and determination. He relied on the kindness of strangers, individuals who, despite their struggles, recognized the yearning for freedom in his eyes. They provided him with shelter, food, and renewed hope. Finally, after weeks of hardship and fear, William reached the promised land of Massachusetts. The moment he crossed the border, the air tasted different, and the sky seemed brighter. He had escaped the clutches of bondage and stepped into the vast unknown of freedom.

### The Quest for Freedom

William's escape was not an isolated incident. It was part of a larger movement, a collective yearning for freedom that swept across the nation. Thousands of enslaved individuals, fueled by the burning desire for a better life, risked everything to break free from the chains of oppression.

The North, although not without its struggles, offered a glimmer of hope. It was a place where people of color could pursue education, own property, and build families without the constant fear of persecution. It was a beacon of liberty, a testament to the power of human strength in the face of oppression.

William's journey was a microcosm of the larger struggle for freedom. It was a testament to the enduring human spirit, a story that continues to inspire generations to fight for a better world. It's a world where freedom is not a privilege but a right everyone enjoys.

William Harvey Carney's early years are a poignant reminder that the human spirit can overcome even the most brutal circumstances. His story proves the power of hope, determination, and the unwavering pursuit of freedom. William's story is a guiding light as humans still grapple with the challenges of inequality and injustice. It reminds you that even in the darkest of times, the flame of freedom is never extinguished.

# The Assault on Fort Wagner: A Heroic Stand

The scorching heat of summer 1863 bore witness to a pivotal moment in American history, the assault on Fort Wagner. This formidable Confederate stronghold, guarding the entrance to Charleston Harbor, became the stage upon which William Harvey Carney would etch his name into the annals of bravery and heroism. His actions on that fateful day transcended mere battlefield valor. They became a potent symbol of defiance, courage, and unwavering belief in the ideals of freedom and equality.

### The 54th Massachusetts Infantry Regiment

Formed in 1863, the 54th Massachusetts Infantry Regiment represented a groundbreaking moment in the history of the United States. This all-Black regiment challenged the deeply ingrained racist beliefs of the time. It served as a tangible embodiment of the fight for equality and justice. The 54th was more than just a military unit. It symbolized hope and a beacon of possibility for enslaved individuals across the nation.

- **Breaking Barriers:** The formation of the 54th shattered the prevailing notion that Black men lacked the courage and capability to serve as soldiers. Their volunteerism amid immense prejudice and skepticism sent a powerful message. It demonstrated their willingness to fight for their freedom and the rights of their people.
- **Challenging Perceptions:** The 54th's battlefield performance silenced critics and proved their mettle as skilled and disciplined soldiers. Their courage and resilience at any cost shattered the deeply ingrained racist stereotypes and paved the way for increased recruitment of Black soldiers throughout the Union Army.
- **A Symbol of Resistance:** The 54th Massachusetts Infantry Regiment transcended military significance. They became a potent symbol of resistance against slavery and a rallying point for abolitionists and freedom seekers nationwide. Their presence on the battlefield challenged the very foundations of the Confederacy and its ideology of racial superiority.

## Assault on Fort Wagner

The assault on Fort Wagner was a desperate gamble. Facing a heavily fortified Confederate position, the 54th Massachusetts Infantry Regiment was tasked with capturing a seemingly impregnable stronghold. The day was filled with chaos, bravery, and immense sacrifices as these brave men charged into the face of enemy fire for a cause they deeply believed in.

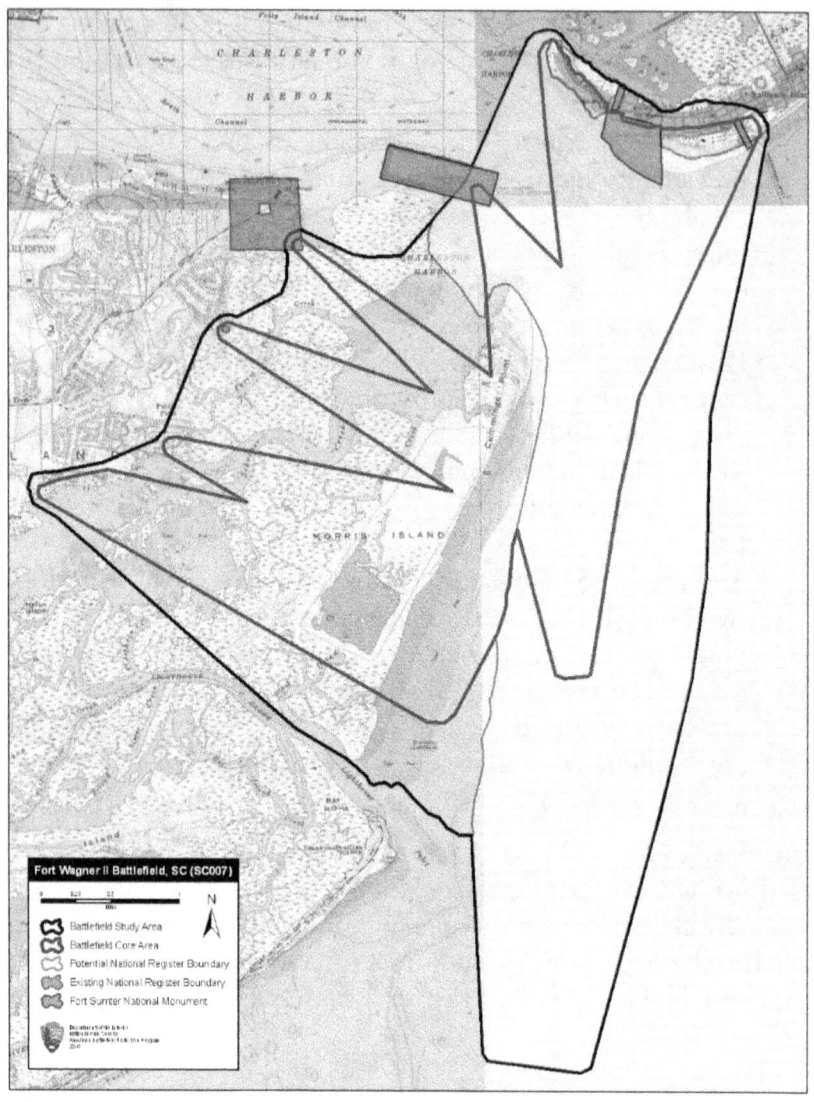

**Map of the Assault on Fort Wagner.**

- **Amidst the Carnage:** The battlefield transformed into a scene of utter chaos. As the 54th advanced, they were met with a hail of bullets and cannon fire. Their comrades fell around them, yet the survivors pressed forward, driven by an unwavering determination and the memory of fallen brothers.
- **Unwavering Bravery:** The 54th displayed extraordinary courage and resilience despite the overwhelming odds. They charged

the fort multiple times, scaling its walls and engaging in hand-to-hand combat. Their bravery at any cost shows the human spirit's capacity for heroism and selflessness.

- **Strategic Significance:** The assault on Fort Wagner, although unsuccessful in capturing the fort, had significant strategic implications. It diverted Confederate troops and resources away from other battlefields, contributing to Union victories elsewhere. Moreover, it highlighted Black soldiers' valor and combat effectiveness, prompting a shift in public opinion and paving the way for greater integration within the Union Army.

### Carney's Unwavering Dedication

In the middle of the chaos and carnage of the battlefield, William Harvey Carney emerged as a symbol of unwavering dedication and heroism. He held the regimental flag high, inspiring his comrades and defying the relentless Confederate fire. His actions transcended mere physical courage. They embodied the fight for freedom and the unwavering belief in the ideals represented by the flag he carried.

- **A Beacon of Hope:** The flag, in Carney's hands, became a rallying point for the 54th Massachusetts Infantry Regiment. It represented the cause they were fighting for, the promise of a future where they would be judged not by the color of their skin but by the nature of their character.
- **Defying the Odds:** Despite being wounded multiple times, Carney refused to abandon the flag. He crawled through the mud and debris, his grip unwavering, his eyes fixed on the fort. His dedication inspired his comrades, urging them to continue the fight in the face of overwhelming odds.
- **A Testament to Freedom:** Carney's actions transcended personal heroism. They represented the fight for freedom and equality for all Americans. His willingness to risk his life for the ideals of the nation served as a powerful counter-narrative to the racist ideologies of the time, demonstrating that Black men were capable soldiers and brave patriots willing to make the ultimate sacrifice for their country.

### Symbolism of the Flag

The American flag, held aloft by William Harvey Carney during the assault on Fort Wagner, carried a profound symbolism that resonated far beyond the battlefield. It became a potent symbol of freedom, equality, and the daily struggles of the racist reality of those days.

- **Defiance of Racist Ideologies**: The American flag, in the hands of a Black soldier, served as a powerful defiance of racist ideologies that deemed Black people inferior and incapable of fighting for their freedom. It challenged the notion that the ideals of liberty and justice represented by the flag did not apply to them.
- **Representation of Hope and Unity:** The flag symbolized hope and unity for the 54th Massachusetts Infantry Regiment. It represented the promise of a future where these soldiers could claim their rightful place as citizens of the United States, free from discrimination and prejudice. It united them in their fight for a common cause, reminding them they were not alone in their struggle.
- **A Call to Action**: The image of Carney carrying the flag was a powerful call to action for the abolitionist movement and supporters of emancipation. It ignited a sense of urgency and highlighted the injustice of slavery, urging them to double their efforts in the fight for freedom.
- **Transcending Boundaries:** The symbolism of the flag transcended the immediate battlefield context. It resonated with Black communities nationwide, offering a glimmer of hope and a sense of empowerment. It became a rallying point for their struggles for freedom and equality, reminding them that the fight for justice was a shared endeavor.
- **A Lasting Legacy:** The image of William Harvey Carney carrying the flag at Fort Wagner remains etched in American memory. It serves as a powerful reminder of the sacrifices made by Black soldiers in the fight for freedom and equality. It continues to inspire generations of Americans to strive for a more just and equitable society where the ideals represented by the flag are a reality for all.

The assault on Fort Wagner may have ended with the 54th Massachusetts being forced to retreat, but the heroic actions of William Harvey Carney left a mark on history. His unwavering dedication to duty, courage in the face of adversity, and belief in the ideals of freedom and equality continue to inspire people today. He is a reminder that even in the darkest times, the human spirit can triumph and that the pursuit of justice and equality is a fight worth fighting.

# Life after War: A Postal Worker and Advocate

The echo of gunfire may have faded from Fort Wagner, but the fire of William Harvey Carney's spirit remained ablaze. He emerged from the battlefield as a decorated hero and a man of conviction and purpose. His story after the Civil War unfolds as a chapter filled with dedication, service, and a fervent pursuit of a better future for himself and his community.

## Postal Worker

The roar of wartime cannons was replaced by the rhythmic clatter of metal mailboxes. William Harvey Carney embarked on a new chapter as a postal worker in New Bedford, Massachusetts. This seemingly ordinary position held profound significance for Carney. It represented a chance to rebuild his life, peacefully contribute to society, and carve a path toward stability after the turmoil of war.

- **Transitioning to a New Landscape:** Discharged from the army in 1865, Carney faced the daunting task of reintegrating into a society while still scarred by the war. He navigated the challenges of discrimination and limited opportunities for African Americans, his resilience shining through in the face of adversity.
- **Building a New Life:** The postal service offered Carney a much-needed haven. He embraced his new role with dedication and professionalism, earning the respect and admiration of his colleagues and the community. This new chapter provided him with a sense of purpose and belonging.
- **Breaking Barriers:** Beyond his achievements, Carney's success paved the way for other African Americans to secure employment in the postal service. He challenged the prevailing prejudices and demonstrated the capabilities of Black individuals, contributing to a more diverse and inclusive workforce.
- **Connecting the Community:** As he walked his daily route, Carney became a familiar face, a friendly presence in the lives of countless individuals. He delivered more than just mail. He delivered kindness, connection, and a sense of community that transcended racial barriers.

## Speeches and Advocacy

The battlefield may have silenced his weapon, but William Harvey Carney's voice remained a powerful force for change. He became a sought-after speaker, captivating audiences with his accounts of heroism and courage during the war. However, his platform extended far beyond personal anecdotes, serving as a springboard for a broader vision of justice and equality.

- **Sharing His Story**: Carney's vivid descriptions of the 54th Massachusetts' bravery shattered stereotypes and challenged the prevailing narratives surrounding Black soldiers. He brought their stories to life, reminding audiences of their sacrifices and vital role in the war effort.

- **A Voice for Equality:** His powerful words transcended the battlefield, addressing the burning issues of civil rights and equality in post-war America. He became a voice for the voiceless, speaking out against discrimination and urging his listeners to strive for a society where justice and opportunity were not privileges but fundamental rights.

- **Sparking Conversations**: Carney's speeches ignited conversations about race and social justice, inspiring generations to take up the mantle of activism. He challenged the status quo, reminded people of the unfinished work of the Civil War, and ignited a passion for building a more just and equitable nation.

- **A Legacy of Advocacy:** His commitment to advocacy extended beyond the podium. He remained active in veterans' organizations, fighting for the rights and recognition of his fellow soldiers. He ensured their sacrifices were not forgotten and advocated for the benefits they deserved.

## Community Engagement

William Harvey Carney never confined himself to the battlefield or the public platform. He actively engaged with his community, recognizing the importance of empowering the next generation and fostering a foundation for a brighter future. His dedication to mentorship, community service, and collaboration left a mark on the lives of countless individuals.

- **Mentoring the Next Generation**: Carney recognized the importance of guiding and supporting young people. He served as a mentor, instilling in them the values of courage, resilience, and the pursuit of justice. He provided guidance, encouragement, and a role model they could strive to emulate.

- **Building a Strong Foundation:** Committed to the advancement of his community, Carney actively supported initiatives focused on education and opportunity for young African Americans. He understood that knowledge and empowerment were key to overcoming challenges and achieving progress.
- **Promoting Unity and Collaboration:** Recognizing the power of unity, Carney actively fostered collaboration between various organizations and groups within the African-American community. He encouraged them to work together towards common goals, building a stronger and more resilient community in the process.
- **Leaving a Lasting Impact:** Through his tireless efforts, Carney left a lasting legacy on his community and beyond. He inspired countless individuals to become involved, contribute to the greater good, and carry the torch of justice and equality forward. His story continues to serve as a beacon of hope and a reminder of the power of individual action in creating a better world.

William Harvey Carney's post-war life reveals a man of exceptional character whose spirit extended far beyond the battlefield. He transitioned seamlessly from decorated hero to dedicated postal worker, his commitment to service and community remaining steadfast throughout his life. His powerful speeches and advocacy for equality challenged the status quo and ignited a passion for justice in countless individuals. As a mentor and community leader, Carney actively empowered young people and fostered a strong foundation for the future.

# Legacy of Service: Medal of Honor and Beyond

William Harvey Carney's legacy is built on courage, perseverance, and dedication to justice. He transcended the battlefield of Fort Wagner, leaving his mark on American history with his actions in the face of enemy fire and through the recognition he received. His service had a lasting impact on subsequent generations.

## Medal of Honor

William Harvey Carney's bravery at Fort Wagner was undeniable, yet his journey to recognition was long and arduous. Decades passed before he received the Medal of Honor, the highest military honor for heroism, due to the pervasive racial prejudices of the time. However, in 1900, his valor finally received its due recognition, marking a significant turning point in American history.

- **Circumstances and Recognition:** The path to recognition was paved by the unwavering dedication of Carney's comrades from the 54th Massachusetts Infantry Regiment. Their relentless campaign ultimately led to President William McKinley bestowing Carney the Medal of Honor in 1900, finally granting him the recognition he deserved.
- **Contemporary Reactions:** The award of the Medal of Honor to William Harvey Carney was a watershed moment, but it wasn't met with universal acclaim. While some celebrated his heroism and saw it as a testament to the courage of Black soldiers, others remained skeptical, reflecting the deeply ingrained biases of the time.
- **Immediate and Long-Term Significance:** Despite the mixed reactions, Carney's recognition had a profound impact. It challenged the prevailing racist ideologies, giving hope to African Americans and opening doors for other Black soldiers to receive the recognition they deserve for their service. This legacy continues to inspire generations, reminding you that courage and perseverance overcome even the most deeply entrenched prejudices.

## Lasting Impact

The ripples of William Harvey Carney's bravery extended far beyond the battlefield and the confines of military service. His story served as a powerful symbol of stability and defiance, inspiring countless individuals and influencing the perception of African-American soldiers throughout history.

- **Perception of African-American Soldiers:** Before Carney's recognition, Black soldiers were often portrayed through a prejudiced lens, deemed incapable and unworthy of the same respect and recognition as their White counterparts. However, Carney's heroism shattered these stereotypes, showcasing Black soldiers' exceptional courage and dedication.

- **Contribution to Civil Rights:** William Harvey Carney's life story became integral to the broader struggle for civil rights. His fight for recognition and equality resonated deeply with the African-American community, providing inspiration and a reminder that the fight for justice was far from over. His legacy continues to motivate activists and advocates in their pursuit of equality and inclusion.

### Commemoration and Recognition

William Harvey Carney's memory and achievements have been commemorated and recognized through various initiatives, ensuring his story endures and continues to inspire future generations.

- **Posthumous Recognition:** Numerous schools, streets, and parks have been named in his honor, and his story is incorporated into educational curriculums across the country. In 2017, the United States Postal Service further solidified his legacy by issuing a commemorative stamp in his honor, ensuring his contributions remain etched in American memory.
- **Monuments and Education:** Physical tributes to William Harvey Carney stand tall as testaments to his heroism. His statue in New Bedford, Massachusetts, and the bust on the grounds of the Massachusetts State House were constant reminders of his bravery and inspired future generations to learn about his life and achievements.
- **Events and Observances:** Throughout the year, events and observances are held to celebrate William Harvey Carney's legacy. Memorial services, educational programs, and community gatherings honor his memory and ensure his story continues to inspire and educate people of all ages.

William Harvey Carney's legacy is not simply a story of battlefield heroism. It portrays the human spirit's capacity for courage, strength, and the unwavering pursuit of justice. He reminds you that even the smallest acts of bravery have far-reaching consequences and that the fight for equality is a continuous journey. By learning from his inspiring life and actively engaging in the fight for a more just society, you'll honor his legacy and ensure that his story continues to inspire generations to come.

This chapter reiterates the overarching theme of courage woven throughout Carney's life. His journey, from enslavement to holding the flag high at Fort Wagner, epitomizes the enduring spirit of those who fought for freedom and equality during a tumultuous period in American history. Carney's legacy extends beyond the pages of this chapter, leaving its mark on the nation's collective memory and standing as a testament to the power of individual courage in shaping the course of history.

# Chapter 5: Dr. Mary Edwards Walker: The Only Woman to Win the Medal of Honor

In the pages of history, Dr. Mary Edwards Walker's story symbolizes courage and challenging societal norms. This chapter emphasizes her groundbreaking contributions as a medical professional, a pioneering feminist, and the only woman to be honored with the Medal of Honor during the Civil War.

Dr. Mary Edwards Walker was the only woman honored with the Medal of Honor during the Civil War.

# Early Life: A Determined Path to Medicine

Dr. Mary Edwards Walker's extraordinary life was not predestined by privilege or circumstance. Instead, it was forged by a determined spirit and a passion for healing that ignited within her early years. To understand the remarkable woman who defied societal norms and shattered barriers in the medical field, you must first explore the formative experiences that shaped her journey.

### Childhood Influences

Mary's formative years were steeped in the rich tapestry of a family deeply invested in education and social justice. Her parents, Alvah and Vesta Whitcomb Walker, instilled in their children a fervent belief in human potential and the importance of education as a tool for empowerment. Growing up on a farm in upstate New York, Mary witnessed firsthand the hardships faced by her community, particularly the lack of access to proper healthcare. It ignited a spark within her, a desire to alleviate suffering and contribute to the well-being of others.

Her family environment further nurtured her burgeoning interest in medicine. Her mother, a trained nurse, shared her knowledge and provided practical guidance, while her sister, Alice, later became a successful physician herself. Surrounded by strong female role models who defied societal expectations, Mary absorbed the message that women possessed the intelligence and capacity to excel in any field, including the traditionally male-dominated field of medicine.

### Pursuit of a Medical Degree

Despite the support of her family, Mary's path to becoming a doctor was fraught with challenges. In the mid-19th century, the doors of medical schools remained largely closed to women. Prejudice and societal expectations confined women to domestic roles, denying them the opportunity to pursue professional careers. Undeterred, Mary refused to be bound by these limitations.

Fueled by her determination, she embarked on her educational journey. She began by attending local academies and seminaries, excelling in her studies, and demonstrating a natural aptitude for science and mathematics. However, her ambitions extended beyond these confines. She yearned to acquire the knowledge and skills necessary to become a physician, a path deemed impossible by many.

Facing numerous rejections and encountering blatant discrimination, Mary refused to be discouraged. Her tenacity eventually led her to Syracuse Medical College in 1855. However, even within the halls of academia, she faced hostility and prejudice. Many male students and professors refused to acknowledge her presence, dismissing her ambitions as mere whims. Yet, Mary persevered, drawing strength from her unwavering belief in herself and her calling.

### Trailblazing Academic Moments

Amidst the challenges, Mary's brilliance and dedication shone through. She excelled in her coursework, consistently ranking among the top students in her class. Her thirst for knowledge and understanding led her to delve deeper into the intricacies of medicine, pushing the boundaries of her education.

One such example was her participation in an anatomy class – initially closed to female students. Mary petitioned the dean and ultimately secured permission to attend, demonstrating her courage and commitment to her studies. This moment marked a significant victory, paving the way for future generations of women to pursue medical careers without facing such barriers.

Another testament to Mary's academic achievements was her groundbreaking thesis, "The Female Physician: A Contribution to the Solution of the Woman Question of the Nineteenth Century." This work challenged the prevailing notion that women were physically and mentally unfit for the demanding field of medicine. It presented a compelling argument for women's inclusion in the medical profession, emphasizing the unique contributions they could make to healthcare and society as a whole.

By defying limitations and achieving academic excellence, Mary Walker carved her path in the medical field and opened doors for countless other women who followed in her footsteps. Her determination, intellectual prowess, and commitment to her calling paved the way for a future where women could contribute their talents and expertise to the advancement of medicine and society.

Dr. Mary Edwards Walker's journey to becoming a doctor was a testament to the power of human ambition and the potential for individual courage to reshape the very fabric of society. From her early experiences to her groundbreaking academic achievements, she defied societal expectations and shattered barriers, paving the way for future generations of women to pursue their dreams in the field of medicine. Her determination and passion for healing continue to inspire women to challenge the status quo and strive for a world where equality and opportunity are fundamental rights for all.

# Volunteer Surgeon for the Union Army: Defying Gender Norms

Dr. Mary Edwards Walker was a woman who defied expectations. Not content to remain confined by the limitations of her time, she embraced the role of a volunteer surgeon during the Civil War. Dr. Walker shattered gender norms and reshaped the narrative of women's contributions to wartime efforts. Her courage extended beyond textbooks and onto the bloodied battlefields, where she served with unwavering dedication and exceptional skill.

### Enlisting as a Surgeon

Driven by a sense of duty and compassion, Dr. Walker refused to sit idly while her nation was embroiled in conflict. Despite initially being denied a formal commission due to her gender, she was undeterred. Determined to make a difference, she volunteered her services and donned civilian attire, often dressing as a man to blend in and gain access to battlefields.

Dr. Walker's dedication to her patients never faltered in the face of skepticism and prejudice. She tirelessly treated the wounded under fire, demonstrating her expertise and composure in the most challenging situations. Her medical skills, honed through years of study and practice, saved countless lives and earned her the respect and admiration of soldiers and commanders alike.

One such example of her courage and skill was during the First Battle of Bull Run in 1861. Caught amidst the chaos and confusion of the battlefield, Dr. Walker calmly and efficiently treated the wounded, earning the praise of General William Tecumseh Sherman, who remarked on her "invaluable services" and "remarkable coolness under fire."

# Challenges and Triumphs: Service in Key Battles

Dr. Walker's service extended beyond a single battle. She volunteered at various battlefields throughout the war, including Fredericksburg, Chancellorsville, and Chattanooga. Facing the horrors of war firsthand, she treated a multitude of injuries, from gunshot wounds to amputations, demonstrating remarkable skill and adaptability in the face of ever-changing circumstances.

At Fredericksburg, amid heavy artillery fire, Dr. Walker tended to the wounded with unwavering resolve. Her calm demeanor and reassuring presence brought comfort and hope to soldiers during their darkest hours. In Chattanooga, she established a field hospital and worked tirelessly to provide care for the injured, her tireless efforts saving countless lives.

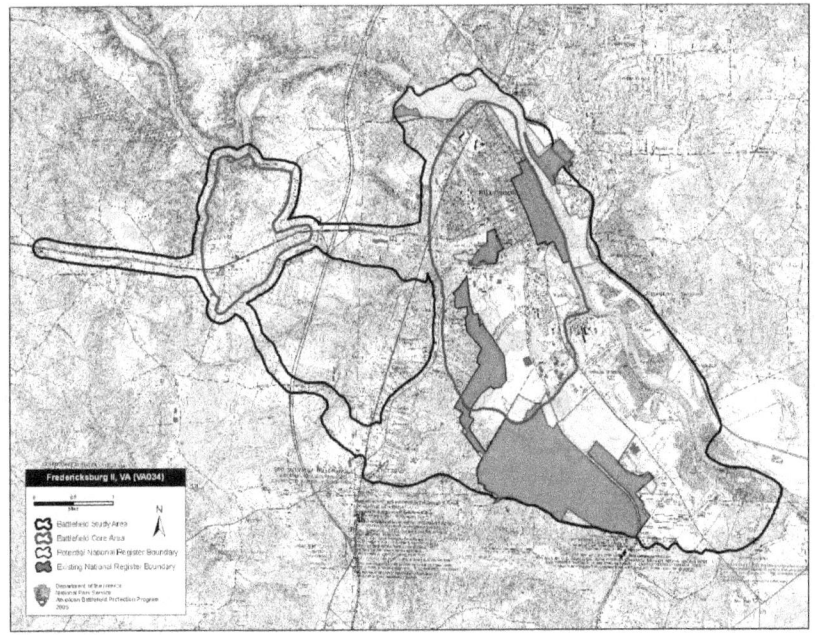

Map of Fredericksburg battlefield.

Dr. Walker's contributions went beyond the battlefield itself. Recognizing the importance of sanitation and hygiene, she advocated for improved hygiene practices and hospital conditions, significantly reducing the risk of infection and saving countless lives. Her innovative approach and dedicated leadership demonstrably improved medical care for Union soldiers.

# Captivity as a POW: Womanhood Amidst Hardships

Dr. Walker's resilience was tested to its limits when she was captured by Confederate forces in 1864. As a prisoner of war, she endured harsh conditions and faced discrimination based on her gender. However, even in captivity, she remained undaunted and continued to provide medical care to her fellow prisoners, her compassion and dedication shining through the darkness.

Dr. Mary Edwards Walker's service as a volunteer surgeon during the Civil War showed courage, skill, and resilience. She defied societal expectations and shattered gender norms, proving that women were capable of serving their country with distinction and expertise.

# Post-War Advocacy: Unconventional Attire and Suffrage

Dr. Mary Edwards Walker's remarkable journey extended far beyond the battlefields of the Civil War. In the post-war era, she continued to challenge societal expectations and blaze a trail for women's rights. She became a renowned advocate for suffrage and defied gender norms through her unconventional attire.

### Defying Gender Expectations

Dr. Walker's post-war years were noted for her distinctive fashion choices. She often wore trousers, a garment considered "masculine" at the time, and rejected the restrictive clothing styles expected of women. Her attire sparked controversy and ridicule, with many viewing it as a deliberate affront to societal norms.

However, Dr. Walker's sartorial choices were far more than mere eccentricity. They represented a conscious rebellion against the constraints placed upon women in the 19th century. By refusing to conform to conventional dress codes, she challenged the very foundations of gender roles and expectations. Her attire symbolized her independence, self-reliance, and unwavering belief in women's equality.

Despite constant criticism and ridicule, Dr. Walker remained unapologetic about her attire. She believed in the freedom of expression and the right of women to dress according to their preferences and needs. Her refusal to be dictated by societal expectations inspired countless women to question the limitations imposed upon them and embrace their individuality.

The impact of Dr. Walker's rebellion extended beyond fashion. It challenged the very definition of what it meant to be a woman in 19th-century America. Her unconventional attire sparked conversations about gender roles, prompting a reevaluation of the prescribed expectations for femininity. Though often ridiculed during her lifetime, Dr. Walker's fashion choices paved the way for a future where women could express themselves freely and defy traditional gender norms without fear of censure.

### Advocacy for Women's Suffrage

Dr. Walker's unwavering belief in equality extended beyond her attire. She became a staunch advocate for women's suffrage, dedicating a significant portion of her life to the fight for women's right to vote.

She actively participated in numerous suffrage campaigns, delivering impassioned speeches and organizing rallies across the country. Her medical expertise and wartime service gave her a unique platform to advocate for women's rights, challenging the notion that women lacked the intelligence and capacity to participate in the political process.

Dr. Walker formed close alliances with other prominent suffragists, such as Susan B. Anthony and Elizabeth Cady Stanton. Together, they strategized, campaigned, and faced arrest for their activism. Dr. Walker's unwavering determination and commitment to the cause inspired countless others to join the fight for suffrage.

Beyond her public advocacy, Dr. Walker utilized her medical skills to directly impact the lives of women. She provided free medical care to women in need and established clinics aimed at improving women's health and well-being. By combining her medical expertise with her commitment to social justice, Dr. Walker created a powerful model for advocating for women's rights and improving their lives.

### Balancing Medicine and Activism

Dr. Walker successfully navigated the complex world of medicine and activism, seamlessly integrating her professional expertise with her dedication to social justice. She continued to practice medicine throughout her life, treating patients from all walks of life. Her compassion and dedication to her patients earned her the respect and admiration of the communities she served.

Dr. Walker used her platform as a physician to promote important reforms related to women's health and well-being. She advocated for improved access to healthcare for women and spoke out against the harmful practices and injustices women faced within the medical system. By combining her medical knowledge with her passion for activism, she created a powerful force for change in the lives of countless women.

Throughout her life, Dr. Walker refused to be confined by societal expectations. She challenged the status quo, fought for equality, and left an enduring legacy as a trailblazer for women's rights. Her unconventional attire, advocacy for suffrage, and the successful balancing act between medicine and activism continue to inspire generations of women to challenge the status quo and fight for a more just and equitable society.

# The Medal of Honor: Recognition and Defiance

Dr. Mary Edwards Walker's exceptional life story reached its pinnacle when she was awarded the Medal of Honor, the highest military honor for bravery in combat. This award was more than a recognition of her heroism. It was a bold act of defiance against the deeply ingrained gender norms of the time.

### The Medal of Honor: Recognition for Service

Dr. Walker's wartime contributions remained largely unrecognized for decades after the Civil War. Despite facing prejudice and discrimination due to her gender, she had tirelessly served as a volunteer surgeon, tending to the wounded on battlefields and enduring harsh conditions as a prisoner of war. However, her dedication and expertise were finally acknowledged in 1917 when Congress awarded her the Medal of Honor for her "meritorious services in dressing the wounded under fire."

This recognition sparked a range of reactions. While some celebrated Dr. Walker's achievements, others remained skeptical, reflecting the deeply ingrained societal biases against women. However, the significance of the award was undeniable. It marked a turning point in American history, acknowledging women's vital role in wartime efforts and challenging the prevailing notion that they were incapable of serving their country with distinction.

## Symbol of Defiance

Dr. Walker's Medal of Honor became much more than a personal accolade. It transformed into a powerful emblem of defiance, challenging the very foundation of gender norms and expectations. As the only woman to ever receive the Medal of Honor, she stood as a stark reminder that bravery, courage, and patriotism were not exclusive traits of men.

Her presence in a sea of male recipients was a constant reminder that women were capable of exceptional service and sacrifice. It shattered the pervasive stereotypes that relegated women to the domestic sphere. It ignited a spark of hope and possibility within countless female hearts, inspiring them to break barriers and pursue their dreams in traditionally male-dominated fields.

Dr. Walker's defiance extended beyond her attire and her wartime service. She openly criticized the military's restrictive policies towards women, advocating for greater opportunities and recognition for their contributions. Her voice and belief in equality paved the way for future generations of women to challenge the status quo and demand their rightful place within the armed forces.

## Influence on Women in Service

Dr. Mary Edwards Walker's legacy continues to resonate within the military as a source of inspiration and encouragement for women pursuing careers in the armed forces. Her story is incorporated into military training programs, ensuring her courage and dedication are not forgotten.

Numerous female military personnel credit Dr. Walker as a personal inspiration, citing her groundbreaking achievements as a motivating factor in their journeys. Her courage in the face of adversity and unwavering commitment to her patients are reminders of the potential and capabilities of women in the military.

In 2016, the United States Army established the Mary Walker Award, recognizing the achievements of female soldiers who demonstrate exceptional courage and commitment to their patients. This award continues to honor her legacy and inspire future generations of women to serve their country with distinction.

# Legacy and Reflections: A Pioneer Remembered

Dr. Mary Edwards Walker's life was not a mere footnote in history. It was a vibrant tapestry woven with courage, defiance, and dedication to equality. Her journey, marked by remarkable achievements and relentless pursuit of justice, continues to inspire generations long after her passing.

### Commemorations and Memorials

Dr. Walker's legacy is etched in historical records, and the physical tributes as testaments to her extraordinary life. Statues and plaques adorn public spaces, reminding you of her contributions and the challenges she overcame. Schools, streets, and even a hospital bear her name, ensuring that her story continues to be told and her memory preserved.

In 1982, the United States Postal Service issued a commemorative stamp in her honor, further solidifying her place in the nation's collective memory. Additionally, numerous organizations dedicated to gender equality and women's rights have established awards and scholarships in her name, inspiring future generations to follow in her footsteps.

These tangible reminders are powerful symbols of Dr. Walker's significance and ensure that her story remains alive in the public consciousness. They honor her achievements and inspire you to continue the fight for the ideals she championed.

### Influence on Future Generations

Dr. Walker's life inspires women across diverse fields. She shattered glass ceilings and defied societal expectations, paving the way for generations of women to pursue their dreams in medicine, the military, and countless other areas once deemed inaccessible.

Her story resonates deeply with those seeking to challenge the status quo and break down barriers. Her commitment to her patients and her fearless advocacy for women's rights continue to motivate individuals and organizations to fight for equality and justice.

Dr. Walker's influence extends beyond individual lives. It shapes contemporary conversations about gender equality, women in medicine, and the broader struggle for civil rights. Her legacy informs discussions about healthcare access, equal pay, and the inclusion of diverse voices in leadership positions.

# Unfinished Battles: The Ongoing Struggle

While Dr. Walker achieved significant milestones in her lifetime, her story confirms that the fight for equality continues, even today. The struggles she faced, the prejudices she challenged, and the battles she fought are a stark reminder that the path toward a truly just society is paved with ongoing challenges.

In today's world, women still confront issues of discrimination and unequal access to opportunities. The fight for full representation in leadership roles, equal pay for equal work, and access to healthcare continue. Dr. Walker's life reminds you that these challenges are not insurmountable and that each individual has the power to contribute to progress.

By reflecting on her triumphs and struggles, you draw inspiration and courage to face the challenges of your own time. Her story reminds you that the fight for equality requires constant vigilance, unwavering commitment, and a collective spirit of resistance against injustice.

Dr. Mary Edwards Walker was more than just a woman ahead of her time. She was a pioneer who shaped the future for generations to come. Her legacy portrays the power of human determination and the potential for individual action to reshape the very fabric of society. By remembering her story and honoring her achievements, we continue to strive for a world where equality and justice are not distant aspirations but a lived reality for everyone.

# Chapter 6: Martin Delany: The Highest Ranking African American

Martin Delany was a polymath who had an impact on war, abolitionism, medicine, and the quest for Black self-determination. This chapter explores the complex story of Delany's life, accentuating his multifaceted role as a soldier, abolitionist, physician, and one of the earliest advocates of Black Nationalism.

Martin Delany was a polymath who had an impact on war.
*https://commons.wikimedia.org/wiki/File:Major_Martin_Delany.jpg*

# Early Years: A Scholar and Abolitionist

Born into a society divided by race and bound by the chains of slavery, Martin Delany's early years were full of intellectual curiosity. He showed a burgeoning passion for dismantling the shackles that held his people captive. Through self-education, early activism, and aspirations in medicine, Delany laid the foundation for a life dedicated to fighting for equality and justice.

### Educational Foundations: From Apprentice to Autodidact

Delany's early education was far from conventional. Born free in Charles Town, Virginia (now West Virginia) in 1812, he moved to Pittsburgh with his mother at the tender age of ten to escape the oppressive laws restricting the education of Black children. This move marked the beginning of Delany's transformative journey, exposing him to a world of intellectual possibilities. It ignited a thirst for knowledge that would fuel his lifelong pursuit of learning.

While apprenticed to a physician, Delany embraced every opportunity to educate himself. He devoured books, learned Latin and Greek, and honed his writing and public speaking skills. He attended lectures and debates, absorbing the ideas of prominent abolitionists and intellectuals like Frederick Douglass and William Lloyd Garrison.

However, Delany's path to becoming a self-taught scholar was not without its obstacles. Racial prejudice and limited access to formal education presented constant challenges. Yet, Delany transformed himself from an apprentice to an autodidact through sheer determination and a relentless pursuit of knowledge. He laid the intellectual foundation for his future as a leading abolitionist, author, and activist.

### The Abolitionist Awakening: Early Activism and Advocacy

Delany's early exposure to the horrors of slavery and the injustices faced by his people ignited a passion for abolitionism that would define his life's work. He began his activist journey in Pittsburgh, writing articles for abolitionist newspapers and engaging in public debates. His powerful voice and eloquent writing quickly gained recognition, establishing him as a prominent figure in the abolitionist movement.

Delany's early activism was not confined to rhetoric. He actively participated in various abolitionist activities, including organizing fundraising campaigns, supporting the Underground Railroad, and advocating for political action. He believed that dismantling slavery required a multifaceted approach, combining intellectual discourse with practical action and political engagement.

Delany's unique perspective as a Black man born free and educated in the North offered a fresh voice within the abolitionist movement. He challenged the prevailing racist ideologies and advocated for a more inclusive approach that recognized the diversity of experiences and perspectives within the Black community.

### Medical Aspirations: The Journey to Becoming a Physician

Delany's early years opened up a deep interest in medicine. He saw it as a powerful tool to empower himself and his community, providing healthcare and a platform to challenge racial prejudices within the medical field.

Despite the significant barriers faced by Black individuals aspiring to become doctors in the mid-19th century, Delany pursued his medical education with determination. He apprenticed with physicians, attended lectures and clinics, and even attempted to enroll in medical school, facing rejection due to his race.

While his formal medical education remained incomplete, Delany's pursuit of medical knowledge proved invaluable. He acquired practical skills that enabled him to provide medical care to his community and further solidified his understanding of the societal and health disparities faced by Black Americans.

Delany's medical aspirations, though ultimately unrealized, represent an important facet of his early years. They reflect his desire for self-improvement, his commitment to serving his community, and his unshakeable belief in the power of knowledge as a tool for empowerment and social justice.

Martin Delany's younger years were a crucible during which his intellectual curiosity, passion for abolitionism, and aspirations in medicine were forged. Through self-education, early activism, and a deep desire to improve the lives of his people, Delany laid the foundation for a life that would leave a mark on American history. His journey is a reminder that even the most formidable obstacles can be overcome through dedication and a commitment to justice.

# Civil War Contributions: A Soldier and Field Officer

Martin Delany's contributions to the Civil War were nothing short of transformative. He went beyond simply fighting for the Union. He played a pivotal role in enlisting Black soldiers, ascended to the first African-American field officer rank, and navigated war challenges with strategic brilliance. His actions impacted both military history and the perception of Black Americans in the national consciousness.

### Recruitment Efforts: Enlisting Black Soldiers

Delany's belief in the importance of Black participation in the war drove him to advocate for recruiting Black soldiers. He traveled extensively throughout the North, delivering impassioned speeches and organizing rallies to encourage Black men to enlist. He emphasized the fight for freedom and equality as a key motivator, challenging the prevailing racist notions that deemed Black men unfit for military service.

Delany's efforts faced immense resistance from both the public and within the military itself. Many White Americans remained skeptical of Black soldiers' capabilities, while prejudiced military leaders actively sought to limit their participation. However, Delany persevered through public criticism and bureaucratic hurdles. Ultimately, he played a crucial role in enlisting over 5,000 Black soldiers, forming the 54th Massachusetts Volunteer Infantry Regiment, and contributing significantly to the Union war effort.

The enlistment of Black soldiers was a pivotal moment in American history. It challenged the deeply ingrained racist ideology and demonstrated the capabilities and valor of Black men on the battlefield. Delany's relentless efforts paved the way for the full integration of Black soldiers into the military, a crucial step toward dismantling racial barriers and achieving equality.

### The First African American Field Officer: A Pioneering Appointment

In 1865, Delany's dedication and exceptional leadership were recognized with his historic appointment as the first African-American field officer in the U.S. Army. He was commissioned a major in the 52nd U.S. Colored Troops Regiment, evidence of his military prowess and a symbolic victory for the Black community.

This groundbreaking achievement shattered a significant barrier and gave hope to Black Americans throughout the nation. It marked a turning point in the perception of Black leadership, demonstrating that Black men were capable of assuming positions of command and responsibility within the military. Delany's appointment opened doors for future generations of Black officers and became a powerful symbol of progress in the fight for racial equality.

## Military Campaigns and Interactions: Navigating War's Challenges

Delany's involvement in the Civil War extended far beyond recruitment efforts and his historic appointment. He actively participated in various military campaigns, demonstrating strategic thinking and tactical expertise. He commanded troops with distinction, earning the respect and admiration of his fellow soldiers and superiors.

He interacted with prominent military leaders throughout his service, including President Abraham Lincoln and General Ulysses S. Grant. He used his platform to advocate for the fair treatment of Black soldiers and argued for their equal recognition and compensation. His interactions with key figures played a crucial role in shaping policies related to Black troops and ensuring their contributions were acknowledged.

Delany's unique position as a Black officer during the Civil War offered him a valuable perspective on the complexities of the conflict. He witnessed firsthand the valor and resilience of Black soldiers while also confronting the pervasive racism and discrimination that they faced. He navigated these challenges with strength and dignity, serving as an inspiration for his fellow soldiers and a vocal advocate for their rights.

Martin Delany's contributions to the Civil War were multifaceted and impactful. He played a significant role in enlisting Black soldiers, shattering racial barriers by becoming the first African-American field officer, and navigating the complexities of war with strategic brilliance.

Delany's actions helped secure victory for the Union and left a mark on American history. They paved the way for a future where Black Americans could be recognized for their valor, leadership, and contributions to the nation's defense. His story is a powerful reminder of the transformative power of individual courage and unwavering commitment to justice.

# Black Nationalism: Vision for an Independent Black Nation

Martin Delany was a soldier, abolitionist, and physician. He was also a visionary who passionately advocated for Black self-determination and nationhood. His bold ideas for an independent Black nation, articulated in his writings and actions, challenged the prevailing racial order and laid the groundwork for future generations of Black activists and intellectuals.

## The Dream of an Independent Black Nation: Ideals and Influences

Delany's vision for an independent Black nation was not born in a vacuum. It was shaped by the complex combination of personal experience, philosophical influence, and the broader historical context of the mid-19th century. He witnessed the brutality of slavery and the systemic racism that pervaded American society. This exposure fueled his desire for a radical solution, a place where Black people could govern themselves and achieve true freedom.

On an intellectual level, Delany drew inspiration from various sources, including the Haitian Revolution, the writings of Marcus Garvey, and the Pan-African movement. He believed that Black people had the potential and right to establish their independent nation, free from the shackles of racism and oppression.

For Delany, Black Nationalism was more than a political strategy. It was a moral imperative. He believed self-determination was essential for Black people to achieve cultural, economic, and social progress. He saw an independent Black nation as a beacon of hope and a catalyst for global liberation.

## Diplomatic Trip to Nigeria: Seeking Partnerships for Liberation

In 1859, Delany embarked on a momentous journey to Africa, specifically Nigeria. This trip was a deliberate effort to establish diplomatic relations and forge alliances with African leaders. Delany believed that Black liberation required a united front and sought to build bridges between the African diaspora and the continent.

During his time in Nigeria, Delany met with various dignitaries and tribal chiefs, proposing a plan for collaboration. He envisioned joint ventures in trade, education, and military defense, aiming to strengthen the economic and political standing of both the African continent and the Black diaspora.

While his diplomatic efforts were not immediately successful, they laid the groundwork for future Pan-Africanism. His vision of unity and collaboration across the Black world resonated with countless individuals and ultimately contributed to the development of broader movements for Black self-determination.

### Legacy of Black Nationalism: Impact and Critique

Delany's advocacy for Black Nationalism continues to spark debate and inspire reflection. His ideas have influenced generations of Black activists, from those who fought for civil rights to those who continue to advocate for economic and social justice today.

Some scholars argue that Delany's vision for Black Nationalism was ultimately unrealistic, given the vast differences between the Black communities in the Americas and Africa. Others question the practicality of forming a separate Black nation in the modern world.

However, Delany's legacy extends far beyond the feasibility of his specific plan. His unwavering commitment to Black self-determination and his emphasis on the importance of Black identity continue to resonate in contemporary discussions about racial justice and social equality.

Delany's vision reminds you that Black people have the right to define their destiny and chart their course. His ideas continue to challenge you to think critically about race, identity, and the quest for true freedom and equality.

While controversial and complex, Martin Delany's vision for an independent Black nation remains a powerful testament to his unwavering commitment to Black liberation. Delany's legacy inspires and challenges you to envision a world where Black people are free from oppression and empowered to shape their destinies.

# Post-War Advocacy: Journalism, Medicine, and Civil Rights

Following the tumultuous years of the Civil War, Martin Delany's commitment to advancing the rights and opportunities of Black Americans did not wane. He continued to fight for justice and equality through various avenues, including journalism, medicine, and active participation in civil rights movements.

### Journalism Ventures: The North Star and Beyond

Delany's journalistic ventures played a crucial role in amplifying the voices of Black Americans and shaping public discourse on race and equality. He collaborated with prominent figures like Frederick Douglass on publications like The North Star. He contributed insightful articles and editorials that challenged racial prejudice and advocated for fair treatment and full citizenship for Black Americans.

Delany's writing addressed a wide range of issues, from the challenges of reconstruction and the plight of freedmen to the ongoing struggle for voting rights and political representation. He used his platform to educate the public, debunk racist myths, and inspire hope for a future where Black Americans could enjoy the full benefits of American democracy.

His journalistic efforts extended beyond established publications. Delany founded and edited his newspapers, such as The Mystery and The Tribune, providing platforms for diverse voices within the Black community and promoting critical discussion on social and political issues. Through his journalism, Delany gave a powerful voice to Black empowerment and was vital to the broader struggle for civil rights.

### Continued Advocacy for Civil Rights: The Fight Persists

Delany's post-war commitment to civil rights took various forms beyond journalism. He actively participated in numerous movements and initiatives to dismantle racial barriers and achieve equality for Black Americans.

Delany was a vocal critic of the injustices faced by freedmen during Reconstruction, advocating for land redistribution and economic empowerment. He was a delegate to the National Colored Conventions, where he passionately argued for Black political representation and full access to education and social services.

He also worked tirelessly to expose and challenge the resurgence of racial violence and discrimination after the war. He documented cases of lynchings and other acts of brutality, bringing attention to the ongoing struggle for Black lives and demanding justice for victims.

Delany's dedication to the civil rights cause extended beyond national movements. He was a prominent figure in his local community, advocating for fair treatment and equal opportunities for Black residents in Pittsburgh. He established businesses and community organizations to empower Black individuals and foster a sense of collective action.

### Medical Practice: Healing in the Aftermath of War

Delany's post-war journey was not solely defined by activism and journalism. He continued to utilize his medical skills to heal the wounds of war and serve the needs of his community. His practice offered hope and support to Black patients who often faced limited access to healthcare due to racial discrimination.

Delany's medical practice extended beyond treating physical ailments. He recognized the interconnectedness of health and social justice, advocating for improved sanitation, hygiene, and access to healthcare for Black communities. He challenged the prevailing racist ideologies within the medical field, striving to ensure equitable treatment for all patients regardless of their race.

Despite his expertise and dedication, Delany faced numerous challenges as a Black physician in a racially stratified society. He encountered prejudice and discrimination from colleagues and patients alike, highlighting the systemic barriers Black professionals faced in achieving recognition and success.

Despite these obstacles, Delany remained undaunted. He persevered, demonstrating the vital role of Black physicians in addressing the healthcare disparities faced by Black communities. He inspired future generations of Black medical professionals, paving the way for greater inclusivity and equity within the field.

Martin Delany's post-war endeavors were a testament to his unwavering dedication to advancing the rights and opportunities of Black Americans. He left a mark on the struggle for civil rights and racial equality through his journalism, activism, and medical practice. His legacy reminds you of the importance of persistent action, unwavering commitment, and the transformative power of individual voices in the fight for justice. Delany's story inspires future generations to carry the torch of equality and strive for a world where justice prevails for all.

# Legacy of Liberation: Beyond the Civil War Hero

Martin Delany's life transcended the boundaries of a Civil War hero. He was a visionary leader, a tireless advocate for Black liberation, and a pioneer whose ideas and actions continue to resonate with generations seeking racial justice and self-determination.

### Commemorations and Memorials: Preserving a Legacy

Delany's enduring legacy is not just made up of historical accounts. His memory is actively preserved through numerous commemorations and memorials, ensuring his contributions are not forgotten. Schools, streets, and even a historical marker in his hometown of Charles Town, West Virginia, bear his name as constant reminders of his remarkable life.

The Martin R. Delany Museum and Archives in Charles Town houses a treasure trove of documents, artifacts, and personal belongings related to Delany's life and work. This museum is a vital resource for scholars and the public alike, offering a deeper understanding of his multifaceted contributions and bringing his story to life.

Organizations dedicated to promoting Black history and culture frequently recognize Delany's achievements. He is often featured in educational material and historical documentaries, ensuring his legacy inspires and informs contemporary audiences.

### Influence on Black Liberation Movements: A Guiding Light

Delany's vision for Black liberation and self-determination extended far beyond his lifetime. His ideas and actions were a guiding light for subsequent generations of activists and intellectuals who continued the fight for racial justice and social equality.

Delany's commitment to Black self-determination inspired leaders like Marcus Garvey and W.E.B. Du Bois, who adopted and expanded on his ideas. His advocacy for Black Nationalism influenced the development of Pan-Africanism, a movement that continues to unite people of African descent globally.

Moreover, Delany's emphasis on education and economic empowerment as pathways to liberation continues to resonate in contemporary discussions about social justice. His vision of self-reliance and community development remains relevant in the quest for equitable access to education, employment opportunities, and healthcare for all.

### Lessons for the Present: Relevance in Contemporary Struggles

Delany's struggles and triumphs offer valuable lessons for understanding contemporary societal challenges and navigating the ongoing fight for justice. His bravery, commitment to equality, and strategic approach to tackling complex issues remain an inspiration for activists and leaders today.

Just as Delany challenged the racist ideologies of his time, you must confront the systemic racism and discrimination that persist in today's society. His belief in the power of collective action reminds you of the importance of organizing, mobilizing, and speaking out against injustice.

Delany's emphasis on education and critical thinking reminds you that knowledge is a powerful tool for empowerment. His dedication to lifelong learning and his commitment to sharing his knowledge with others inspire individuals to seek knowledge, engage in critical discourse, and challenge the status quo.

# Chapter 7: Susie King Taylor: From Slave to Nurse

The story of Susie King Taylor speaks volumes about a resilient and multifaceted figure. Her narrative transcends the shackles of slavery to become a beacon of hope and healing during the tumultuous years of the Civil War. This chapter sheds light on Taylor's extraordinary journey from an enslaved child in Georgia to becoming a nurse, educator, and laundress. It draws inspiration from her memoir, "Reminiscences of My Life in Camp," to provide an account of her experiences and the challenges faced by Black troops.

*Susie King Taylor*

**Susie King Taylor was a nurse, educator, and laundress.**
*https://commons.wikimedia.org/wiki/File:Susie_King_Taylor_LCCN2003653538.jpg*

# Early Experiences: Foundations of Resilience

Born into the suffocating grip of slavery in Georgia in 1848, Susie King Taylor's early life led her to develop resilience and an unbreakable spirit. Her childhood, steeped in the harsh realities of slavery, would shape her worldview and ignite a lifelong dedication to freedom and education.

### Enslaved Childhood in Georgia: The Crucible of Bondage

Susie's early years were defined by the hardships and deprivations inherent in slavery. Separated from her mother at a young age, she grew up on the Grest plantation in Liberty County, Georgia, surrounded by the daily injustices and brutalities of the system. The dehumanization and exploitation she witnessed firsthand instilled in her a deep understanding of the cruelties inflicted on enslaved individuals and fueled a burning desire for freedom.

Despite the challenges, Susie's childhood was not devoid of tenderness. Her loving grandmother, Dolly, provided a haven of warmth and solace amidst the harsh realities of their lives. Dolly nurtured Susie's curiosity and encouraged her to learn, instilling in her a thirst for knowledge that would become a defining characteristic.

The bonds of family, though often fractured and fragile, remained a source of strength for Susie. She found solace and support in her siblings, sharing stories, dreams, and aspirations in the hushed spaces of nighttime gatherings. These moments of connection provided a glimmer of hope in the darkness of their enslaved existence.

### Clandestine Education: Nurturing the Seeds of Knowledge

In defiance of the laws that prohibited enslaved people from learning to read and write, Susie embarked on a clandestine journey of self-education. She learned the alphabet by tracing letters in the dirt, seizing every opportunity to glean knowledge from scraps of paper or discarded books.

Her thirst for knowledge led her to seek out secret schools run by brave Black women who risked their freedom to educate their people. Within these clandestine classrooms, Susie's mind was ignited. She devoured books, sharpened her writing skills, and learned history, geography, and mathematics.

This clandestine education was a transformative experience for Susie. It empowered her to see the world through new eyes, to understand the injustices she endured, and to dream of a future free from bondage.

Education became her weapon, a tool for empowerment and self-discovery that would fuel her future activism.

### The Road to Freedom: Escape and a New Beginning

At the young age of sixteen, Susie seized the opportunity to escape from slavery. The details of her escape remain shrouded in mystery, but it is clear that it was a courageous act fueled by her burning desire for freedom.

Her journey to freedom was fraught with danger and uncertainty. Navigating the perilous terrain of the South, she faced the constant threat of capture and the ever-present fear of being returned to the horrors of slavery. Despite the challenges, Susie persevered. Her resilience, nurtured during her childhood, propelled her forward. She relied on her wit, intelligence, and the kindness of strangers to find her way to freedom.

Finally, Susie reached freedom in the North, a land where she could finally breathe the air of liberty without fear. This new chapter in her life marked a turning point. She was no longer a slave but a free woman with a boundless spirit and a determination to make a difference in the world.

Though marked by hardship and oppression, Susie King Taylor's early experiences laid the foundation for her remarkable life. Her childhood instilled in her a deep understanding of human resilience, while her clandestine education provided her with the knowledge and skills she needed to navigate the complexities of a changing world. As she stepped into the next chapter of her life, she carried with her the scars of her past yet remained undaunted by the challenges that lay ahead.

# The 33rd United States Colored Infantry Regiment: A Commitment to Service

In 1862, Susie King Taylor's life took a pivotal turn when she joined the 33rd United States Colored Infantry Regiment (USCI) during the Civil War. Her association with this regiment would transcend the traditional roles ascribed to Black women during the era. It showcased her remarkable resilience, multifaceted contributions, and unwavering commitment to service.

## Educator amid War: Teaching Black Soldiers

While officially enlisted as a laundress, Susie recognized the immense need for education among the newly recruited Black soldiers. Many of these men had been denied basic literacy and numeracy skills due to the systemic oppression of slavery. Recognizing this gap, Susie stepped forward as an educator, teaching at night despite the hardships of camp life.

Her makeshift classroom, often illuminated by the flickering light of a campfire, became a sanctuary for learning and empowerment. Taylor's dedication to education transcended the limitations of resources and time. She used whatever materials she could find, from discarded newspapers to handwritten notes, to impart valuable knowledge and instill a sense of self-worth in her students.

MY SCHOOLHOUSE IN SAVANNAH

**Susie King Taylor's schoolhouse in Savannah.**
*https://commons.wikimedia.org/wiki/File:Susie_King_Taylor_School.jpg*

Beyond literacy and numeracy, Susie also taught her students about history, geography, and current events. She encouraged them to engage in critical thinking and discussions, fostering a sense of awareness and agency that would be crucial for their future lives.

Facing skepticism and prejudice from some, Susie remained undeterred. Her commitment to education was unwavering. She believed that knowledge was the key to empowerment and liberation for individual soldiers and the entire Black community.

### Tending to the Wounded: The Healing Touch of a Nurse

Susie's skills and compassion extended beyond the classroom as the war intensified. She became a dedicated nurse, tending to the wounded on the front lines. Her memoir, "Reminiscences of My Life in Camp with the 33rd United States Colored Troops," offers vivid accounts of the harsh conditions she faced and the emotional toll of caring for soldiers injured in battle.

With limited resources and often under fire, Susie displayed remarkable courage and resilience. She provided medical care, comfort, and support to countless soldiers, offering a beacon of hope and humanity amidst the brutality of war.

Her experiences on the battlefield were deeply impactful. Witnessing the suffering and loss firsthand strengthened her resolve to fight for a world free from oppression and injustice.

### Camp Logistics and Laundress Duties: Sustaining the Regiment

Beyond her roles as an educator and nurse, Susie also played a vital role in the regiment's daily operations. She contributed significantly to camp logistics, ensuring the smooth running of essential services like food preparation and sanitation.

She also fulfilled her official duties as a laundress, ensuring the cleanliness and hygiene of the soldiers' uniforms. This seemingly mundane task was crucial for maintaining morale and preventing the spread of disease.

By diligently performing these seemingly disparate roles, Susie embodied the spirit of service and selflessness that characterized the 33rd USCI. She recognized that every contribution, regardless of its nature, was vital to the overall success and well-being of the regiment.

Susie King Taylor's service with the 33rd USCI regiment showcased her courage, resilience, and dedication to service. She broke through societal barriers, defying traditional gender roles and exceeding expectations. As an educator, nurse, and camp organizer, she was instrumental in supporting the regiment and empowering her fellow soldiers.

More importantly, Susie's life portrayed the potential for human commitment and the transformative power of education and service. Even during the war, she found the strength to uplift others and work toward a better future. Her legacy continues to inspire generations of individuals to challenge societal norms, embrace education, and dedicate themselves to the service of others.

# "Reminiscences of My Life in Camp": A Firsthand Perspective

Susie King Taylor's memoir, "Reminiscences of My Life in Camp with the 33rd United States Colored Troops," offers you a unique and invaluable glimpse into the Civil War era from the perspective of a Black woman serving alongside Black soldiers. Through her words, you'll be transported back in time, witnessing the challenges, triumphs, and enduring humanity of a community fighting for freedom and equality.

### Voices from the Past: Excerpts from "Reminiscences"

Taylor's vivid prose allows you to experience the war through her eyes. You hear the fear in her voice as she describes the chaos of battle: "*The shells and bullets were flying thick and fast, and the men were falling around me like leaves in a storm.*" Her compassion is palpable as she recounts tending to the wounded: "*I saw a young soldier lying on the ground, his leg torn to pieces. I went to him at once and did all I could for him.*"

You'll also witness her unwavering spirit and determination. While acknowledging the hardships faced by Black troops, she writes, "*We were not discouraged, but rather more determined to fight for our freedom.*" Her words resonate with strength and resilience, reminding you of the human capacity to overcome adversity.

### Challenges of Black Troops: Racism, Inequality, and Resilience

Taylor's memoir exposes the stark reality of racism and inequality that Black troops faced during the Civil War. She describes the prejudice they encountered from White officers and the unequal treatment they received in terms of pay, rations, and equipment.

Despite these challenges, Black soldiers demonstrated unwavering courage and dedication. Taylor writes, "*We knew that we were fighting for a cause that was just, and we were determined to win.*" Their bravery and resilience in the face of adversity are proof of their commitment to freedom and equality.

### The Human Side of War: Personal Stories and Struggles

Taylor's memoir goes beyond documenting historical events. It humanizes the war by sharing personal stories and struggles. She paints portraits of individual soldiers, highlighting their hopes, dreams, and fears. You learn about their families back home, their dreams for the future, and the sacrifices they made for their country.

The human cost of the war can be felt through Taylor's accounts. You'll grieve alongside her as she recounts the loss of friends and comrades. You'll feel her frustration and anger at the senselessness of war. Yet, even amidst the darkness, you see glimpses of hope and humanity.

"Reminiscences of My Life in Camp" is more than a historical document. It's a powerful testament to the human spirit. Through Taylor's words, you gain a deeper understanding of the complexities of the Civil War era and the experiences of Black troops who fought for their freedom. Her story reminds you of the importance of fighting for justice and equality, even when facing such great odds.

Taylor's call to action resonates across time: *"Let us not forget the sacrifices made by those who fought for our freedom. Let us continue to fight for justice and equality for all."* Her words inspire you to learn from the past, build a better future, and honor the legacy of those who came before you.

# Post-War Advocacy: A Lifetime of Service

Susie King Taylor's commitment to service did not end with the conclusion of the Civil War. Her spirit of activism and dedication to justice continued to fuel her efforts in the post-war years, as she tirelessly advocated for veterans and championed the cause of women's rights.

### Advocacy for Veterans: The Unfinished Battle

Having witnessed firsthand the sacrifices and struggles of Black soldiers during the war, Taylor remained deeply concerned about their well-being and recognition in the aftermath. She became a vocal advocate for their rights, demanding fair treatment, pensions, and access to their rightfully deserved benefits.

Taylor's post-war advocacy focused on addressing the specific needs of Black veterans. She recognized their unique challenges, including discrimination, limited access to healthcare and education, and widespread unemployment. She actively campaigned for government recognition of their service and fought for the implementation of policies that would ensure economic security and social inclusion.

Taylor's advocacy for veterans was not without its challenges. She faced opposition from both the government and segments of society who sought to minimize the contributions of Black soldiers and deny them the benefits they had earned. Despite these obstacles, she remained undeterred, using her voice and influence to raise awareness and advocate for their needs.

### Women's Organizations: A Voice for Change

Drawing on her experiences during the war and witnessing the limitations placed on women, Taylor became an active participant in the burgeoning women's rights movement. She joined various organizations, including the National Association of Colored Women (NACW), where she found a platform to advocate for women's suffrage and social justice.

Taylor's contributions extended beyond mere membership. She used her writing skills to contribute to women's rights publications, raising awareness about the challenges women of color face and advocating for equal opportunities in education, employment, and political participation.

Her experiences during the war, where she defied societal expectations and served in traditionally male roles, informed her advocacy for women's rights. She believed that women should be able to participate fully in society and contribute their talents and skills without limitations based on gender.

### A Lifelong Legacy of Service: Impact on Generations

Susie King Taylor's lifelong commitment to service continues to inspire generations. Her dedication to veterans and her advocacy for women's rights left a mark on the post-war landscape.

Taylor's efforts contributed significantly to the advancements made in both the Civil Rights movement and the women's suffrage movement. Her advocacy paved the way for greater equality and recognition for Black soldiers and women, inspiring others to fight for justice and challenge discriminatory practices.

Beyond specific movements, Taylor's legacy is a timeless inspiration for all who seek to make a difference in the world. Her courage, resilience, and commitment to service remind you that even one individual makes a profound impact by raising their voice and taking action against injustice.

Susie King Taylor's journey, from her childhood in slavery to her post-war advocacy, provides hope and inspiration. By remembering her life and contributions, you'll continue to strive for a world where justice, equality, and the rights of all individuals are upheld and celebrated.

# Susie King Taylor: A Voice for the Ages

Susie King Taylor was not just a Civil War heroine. She was a vital voice for the experiences of Black Americans during a period of profound transformation. Her life and contributions transcended the battlefield, leaving an enduring legacy that continues to resonate across generations.

### Commemorations and Tributes: Preserving the Legacy

Susie King Taylor's memory is actively preserved through various commemorations and tributes that ensure her story remains etched in the collective consciousness. Schools, streets, and historical markers bear her name, serving as constant reminders of her remarkable life. Her memoir, "Reminiscences of My Life in Camp with the 33rd United States Colored Troops," continues to be a valuable historical resource, offering a firsthand account of the Civil War era and the struggles and triumphs of Black soldiers.

Institutions like the National Park Service and historical societies organize educational programs and events dedicated to Susie King Taylor's life and work. These efforts bring her story to life for new audiences, fostering appreciation for her courage, resilience, and enduring impact.

### Lessons for Today: Relevance in Contemporary Struggles

Susie King Taylor's story offers valuable lessons for navigating contemporary challenges. Her struggles against racism and inequality resonate deeply with ongoing fights for racial justice and social equality. Her commitment to education remains a potent reminder of the importance of knowledge and empowerment in dismantling systemic barriers.

Taylor's journey also highlights the vital contributions of Black women throughout history, often overlooked and under-recognized. Her life shows the strength, intelligence, and leadership of Black women, urging you to acknowledge their multifaceted roles and celebrate their achievements.

By reflecting on the struggles and triumphs of Susie King Taylor, you'll gain a deeper understanding of the ongoing quest for racial equality and social justice. Her story is a source of inspiration for individuals and movements working towards a more just and equitable world.

# The Power of Resilience: An Everlasting Inspiration

Susie King Taylor's life embodies the profound power of resilience. Born into slavery, she faced unimaginable hardships and injustices. Yet, she persevered.

Throughout her life, Susie King Taylor defied limitations and expectations. She embraced education as a tool for liberation, served her community with dedication, and raised her voice against oppression. Her courage and resilience in the face of adversity inspire all who face challenges and strive for positive change.

Susie King Taylor's legacy reminds you that the pursuit of justice and equality is a continuous journey. It requires commitment, strength, and the courage to speak truth to power. By drawing inspiration from her story, you'll continue towards a world where justice prevails and all voices are heard and valued.

### A Testament to Fortitude

As the echoes of Susie King Taylor's remarkable life fade into history, a profound silence descends, inviting you to contemplate its enduring legacy. Her story, a testimony of fortitude and unwavering spirit, transcends the confines of a single life, inspiring future generations.

In the face of unimaginable hardship, Susie King Taylor refused to be defined by the limitations imposed upon her. Instead, she carved her path through the challenges of slavery, war, and societal prejudice. Her pursuit of knowledge, dedication to service, and courage in the face of adversity are potent reminders of the boundless potential that resides within each human spirit.

The echoes of Susie King Taylor's life reverberate with timeless implications. Her journey compels you to confront the injustices that persist in the world, to challenge the systems that perpetuate inequality, and to ignite the flames of change within yourself and your community. Her voice, though silenced by the passage of time, continues to resonate through the ages, urging you to embrace education as a weapon against ignorance, service as a pathway towards collective progress, and resilience as the shield that protects us from despair.

You are presented with a choice as you stand upon the shoulders of giants like Susie King Taylor: succumb to the inertia of the past or carry the torch of her legacy forward. Will you allow the embers of her spirit to fade into obscurity, or will you fan them into a roaring flame that illuminates the path toward a more just and equitable future?

As you honor the memory of Susie King Taylor, remember her not only as a Civil War heroine but as a timeless voice for the experiences of Black Americans. Let her story continue to inspire individuals and communities to embrace education, fight for justice, and strive for a future where the ideals of equality and freedom truly flourish.

# Chapter 8: André Cailloux: The Hero of Port Hudson

Like a luminous thread woven into the complex fabric of Civil War history, Captain André Cailloux stands out as an emblem of unbreakable spirit. His story is one of remarkable transformation, a journey that begins in the shadows of enslavement and culminates in the glorious light of heroic leadership. This chapter explores the intricate tapestry of Cailloux's life, illuminating his remarkable evolution from a young man bound by the chains of slavery in Louisiana to the revered "Hero of Port Hudson," a symbol of African-American bravery and determination in the face of profound adversity.

André Cailloux's life was celebrated by all, even after his death.
*https://commons.wikimedia.org/wiki/File:Caillouxfuneral.jpg*

# Early Years: A Transformation

Born into the suffocating grip of slavery in Louisiana in 1825, André Cailloux's early life started his extraordinary journey. His childhood, steeped in the harsh realities of bondage, would shape his worldview and set the stage for his remarkable transformation into a leader of the free Black community and a staunch advocate for justice and equality.

### Enslavement in Louisiana

Cailloux's early years were marked by the brutality and dehumanization inherent in slavery. He grew up on the Duvernay plantation in Plaquemines Parish, surrounded by the daily injustices and brutalities of the system. Witnessing the inherent cruelty inflicted upon enslaved individuals firsthand fueled a burning desire for freedom and a deep understanding of the injustices that plagued his community.

Despite the hardships, Cailloux's early life was not devoid of moments of warmth and resilience. His family provided a haven of support and love amidst the harsh realities of their existence. His mother, Josephine, instilled in him a strong moral compass and a sense of self-worth that would prove invaluable in his future endeavors.

Cailloux's experiences during his youth were formative. He witnessed the resilience of his fellow slaves, learned the importance of community and solidarity, and developed a deep appreciation for the freedoms that were denied to him. These early experiences became the foundation for his unwavering commitment to justice and equality throughout his life.

### Manumission and Rise in Free Black Community: The Quest for Freedom

In 1846, Cailloux's life took a pivotal turn when he was granted freedom by the Duvernay family. His liberation was a result of his intelligence, hard work, and unwavering spirit. Once free, Cailloux moved to New Orleans, a vibrant hub of free Black life and a center of resistance against slavery.

He quickly established himself as a successful businessman, building a thriving cigar-making business. His entrepreneurial success allowed him to achieve a degree of economic self-sufficiency and provided him with the resources to support his growing family.

Beyond his professional pursuits, Cailloux became deeply involved in the social and political life of the free black community. He joined various organizations dedicated to improving the lives of African

Americans, advocating for educational opportunities and political representation. He also became a vocal critic of slavery and a staunch advocate for its abolition.

Cailloux's rise in the free Black community was marked equally by challenges and opportunities. He faced discrimination and prejudice from White society, but he also found strength and support within his community. He used his influence and resources to uplift others, assisting fellow freed slaves and working tirelessly to improve the overall well-being of his community.

The years following his manumission were a time of significant transformation for Cailloux. He transitioned from a slave to a successful businessman, a community leader, and a vocal advocate for justice. His early experiences in slavery shaped his worldview and fueled his commitment to fighting for a better future for himself and his community.

# Joining the Union Forces: Leadership in the 1st Louisiana Native Guard

In 1861, André Cailloux's life took another pivotal turn. As the embers of the Civil War ignited across the nation, Cailloux, a successful businessman and leader in the New Orleans free Black community, made a momentous decision to join the Union forces. This choice, driven by a complex mix of personal convictions and historical circumstances, made him a pioneering figure in American military history and a symbol of courage and leadership.

### The Call to Arms: Joining the Union Forces

Motivations behind Cailloux's enlistment were multifaceted. Having witnessed the brutality of slavery firsthand, he had a deep desire for freedom and equality. He believed that joining the Union Army presented a unique opportunity to fight for his liberation, the future of his community, and the abolition of a system that had inflicted untold suffering.

Beyond these ideological motivations, Cailloux also recognized the potential for upward mobility and social advancement that military service offered. The Union Army, facing a manpower shortage, was actively recruiting Black soldiers. It was an opportunity to earn a living wage, gain valuable skills, and challenge the racial barriers that had long impeded their progress.

However, Cailloux's decision was not without its complexities. He was a successful businessman with a family and a comfortable life in New Orleans. Joining the army meant leaving behind everything he had built and risking his life in the brutal realities of war. Moreover, the decision to fight for the Union was not universally embraced within the free Black community. Some feared that military service would further endanger their lives and families, while others questioned the Union's commitment to ending slavery.

Despite these doubts and concerns, Cailloux's resolve remained unwavering. He believed the fight for freedom was worth any sacrifice, and he was determined to play his part in achieving a more just and equitable society.

### The 1st Louisiana Native Guard: Pioneers of African-American Military Service

In 1862, Cailloux enlisted in the 1st Louisiana Native Guard, a pioneering regiment composed entirely of Black soldiers. This regiment, the first of its kind in the Civil War, was a testament to the growing recognition of Black soldiers' potential and their vital role in the Union's war effort.

The 1st Louisiana Native Guard faced numerous challenges. Initially, they were not issued proper uniforms or weapons. They were also often relegated to menial tasks like fatigue duty. Additionally, they faced widespread prejudice and discrimination from both Confederate forces and some within the Union ranks.

However, the Native Guard persevered. They proved their courage and fighting prowess in numerous battles, including Port Hudson and Milliken's Bend. Their bravery and skill dispelled racist myths about the capabilities of Black soldiers and paved the way for the integration of Black troops into the Union Army.

# André Cailloux's Leadership: The Rise of a Hero

Cailloux emerged as a natural leader within the 1st Louisiana Native Guard. He quickly rose through the ranks, eventually becoming captain of his company. His leadership was characterized by a combination of strategic acumen, inspiring presence, and dedication to the welfare of his men.

Cailloux's strategic mind was evident in his ability to adapt to battlefield conditions and make quick decisions under pressure. His men loved and respected him for his bravery and willingness to share their hardships. He was known for his calm demeanor and the ability to inspire courage and confidence in his troops.

Beyond his tactical and inspirational qualities, Cailloux was also a dedicated advocate for his soldiers' rights. He actively fought for better treatment and recognition for the Native Guard, challenging prejudice and discrimination within the Union Army. His efforts ensured that Black soldiers were treated with dignity and respect and received the same benefits and opportunities as their White counterparts.

Cailloux's leadership played a pivotal role in the success of the 1st Louisiana Native Guard. He served as more than just a military commander. He was also a mentor, a confidant, and a symbol of hope and resilience for his fellow soldiers. His legacy lives on as a tribute to the courage and leadership of African-American soldiers during the Civil War and their enduring fight for freedom and equality.

André Cailloux's decision to join the Union forces and his subsequent leadership within the 1st Louisiana Native Guard were defining moments in American history. He shattered racial barriers, defied expectations, and emerged as a hero who fought for freedom and justice. His story inspires all who strive for a more equitable world. It reminds you that even the most seemingly insurmountable obstacles can be overcome through courage, determination, and commitment to a noble cause.

# The Assault on Port Hudson: Bravery in the Face of Mortal Injury

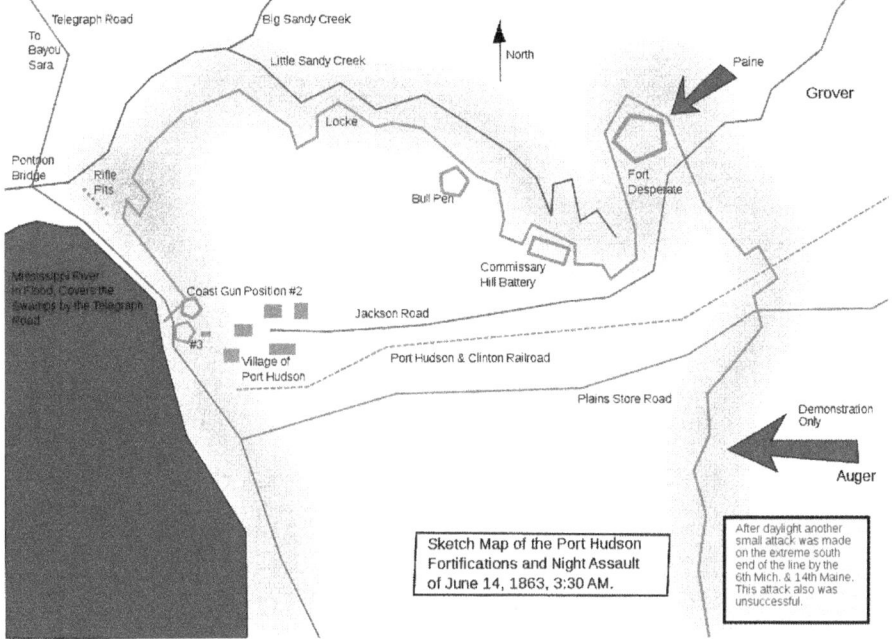

**Map of the Assault on Port Hudson.**
*Calendar5, CC0, via Wikimedia Commons:*
https://commons.wikimedia.org/wiki/File:Port_Hudson_Night_Attack_One.svg

In the summer of 1863, Captain André Cailloux and the 1st Louisiana Native Guard were embroiled in one of the most significant battles of the Civil War. It began with the siege of Port Hudson. This strategic Confederate stronghold on the Mississippi River represented a major obstacle to the Union's efforts to gain control of the waterway and split the Confederacy in two.

## The Strategic Significance of Port Hudson: Setting the Stage

Port Hudson was more than just a fortified town. It was a vital artery for the Confederacy. Its capture would sever critical supply lines and communication channels and deal a morale blow to the South. For the Union, conquering Port Hudson was crucial to achieving their broader war aims.

However, the task was daunting. Confederate forces had meticulously constructed an elaborate network of earthworks, trenches, and artillery positions, making Port Hudson a formidable fortress. The Union, facing heavy casualties in earlier assaults, needed a strategic shift.

### André Cailloux at Port Hudson: Leading the Charge

During this critical juncture, Captain Cailloux stepped forward. With courage and resolute leadership, he rallied his men for a daring assault on the Confederate lines. On May 27, 1863, under a relentless barrage of enemy fire, Cailloux led the charge, inspiring his troops with his unwavering determination and personal bravery.

He led from the front, his voice booming above the din of battle as he urged his men forward. He led the charge through a hail of bullets, undeterred by the casualties mounting around him. His courage and dedication inspired his fellow soldiers, who followed him with loyalty and determination.

Cailloux's leadership extended beyond mere bravery. He displayed a strategic mind, maneuvering his troops through the Confederate defenses and exploiting weaknesses in their lines. He rallied his men when they faltered, rekindled their spirit, and led them forward time after time.

# The Hero's Sacrifice: André Cailloux's Last Stand

Despite his valiant efforts, the assault ultimately failed. Facing overwhelming odds and withering fire, the Union forces were forced to retreat. However, Cailloux refused to yield. He remained on the battlefield, steadfast in his commitment to his mission and determined to protect his men.

Tragically, during this final stand, Cailloux was struck by a Confederate sharpshooter's bullet, mortally wounded. As he lay on the battlefield, surrounded by his fallen comrades, he continued to encourage his soldiers to fight on. His last words, "Let us go forward, for one more time!" echoed through the battlefield.

The death of Captain Cailloux sent shockwaves through the ranks of the 1st Louisiana Native Guard and the broader Union army. He was revered as a hero, a symbol of bravery and sacrifice in the face of insurmountable odds. His legacy was a powerful rallying cry, inspiring his fellow soldiers to continue fighting for freedom and equality.

The assault on Port Hudson was pivotal in the Civil War, and André Cailloux's bravery and leadership were etched into its annals. His courage and dedication to the cause, even in the face of mortal injury, are enduring proof of the spirit of heroism and the sacrifices made in the pursuit of freedom. He was a pioneer, a leader, and a hero whose legacy continues to inspire generations to fight for what is right, even in the face of adversity.

Cailloux's sacrifice was not in vain. Port Hudson eventually fell to Union forces, and the Confederacy was ultimately defeated. His story reminds you that the fight for freedom and equality often demands courage, sacrifice, and unwavering commitment, even in the face of seemingly impossible odds.

### The Public Funeral in New Orleans: A Symbolic Turning Point

In the sweltering heat of July 1863, New Orleans witnessed a spectacle unlike any seen before. Thousands of mourners, predominantly African American, thronged the streets of the city to pay their final respects to Captain André Cailloux, a hero of the Civil War who had fallen just weeks prior during the siege of Port Hudson. This public funeral, an unprecedented display of unity and defiance, became a pivotal moment in American history. It became a powerful symbol of African-American valor, rallying support for Black troops and challenging deeply ingrained prejudices.

### The Symbolism of the Public Funeral: A Hero's Tribute

Cailloux's funeral transcended the somber ritual of mourning. It was a public declaration of pride and a celebration of a life dedicated to freedom and equality. The meticulously planned procession, led by a band playing solemn dirges, stretched for miles, winding through the heart of the city's Black community. Over 30 mutual aid societies participated, their banners and flags waving proudly in the air. The sheer size and solemnity of the event resonated deeply with the African-American community.

Cailloux's funeral also was a direct challenge to the prevailing racist attitudes of the time. By granting him a hero's burial, the community defied the expectations of a society that sought to diminish and erase the contributions of Black soldiers. His casket, draped in the American flag and adorned with his sword and uniform, stood as an assertive symbol of patriotism and sacrifice, demanding recognition for the bravery and valor of African-American troops.

### Impact on Rallying Support: Changing Perceptions

The impact of Cailloux's public funeral extended far beyond the confines of New Orleans. Newspapers nationwide reported on the event, highlighting the unprecedented display of support for a Black soldier. This widespread coverage shifted perceptions about the capabilities and contributions of African-American soldiers, challenging the deeply ingrained stereotypes that portrayed them as inferior and unfit for combat.

The funeral also became a potent tool for recruitment, inspiring other Black men to join the fight for freedom. Seeing the community's outpouring of grief and admiration for Cailloux, many were moved to take up arms and defend the cause of the Union. The success of the 1st Louisiana Native Guard, which Cailloux commanded with distinction, further fueled this momentum, demonstrating the effectiveness of Black troops in combat.

# Legacy of André Cailloux: A Beacon of Courage and Commitment

André Cailloux's life and story embody the spirit of resistance against oppression and the unwavering determination to fight for justice and equality. His public funeral was a testament to the power of collective action and the ability of a community to rise above adversity and demand recognition.

The public funeral of André Cailloux was a turning point in American history. It challenged deeply ingrained racial prejudices and ultimately contributed to the advancement of civil rights and equality. Cailloux's story reminds you that courage, sacrifice, and commitment are essential ingredients in the fight for a more just and equitable world. His legacy inspired generations to stand for what is right and fight for a future where freedom and equality are not aspirations but realities.

### Epilogue: André Cailloux's Enduring Legacy

How does the legacy of this remarkable man translate into the contemporary world? His journey, from the depths of enslavement to the heights of heroism, offers valuable lessons for navigating the complexities of this time.

### Commemorations and Memorials: Preserving a Hero's Memory

The memory of André Cailloux continues to be actively preserved through commemorations and memorials that ensure his story remains etched in the collective consciousness. Schools, streets, and historical markers bear his name as constant reminders of his remarkable life. His image adorns monuments and museums, guaranteeing that his sacrifice is never forgotten.

Organizations like the National Park Service and historical societies dedicate programs and events to honoring Cailloux's legacy. These efforts bring his story to life for new audiences, fostering appreciation of his courage, resilience, and the enduring impact his life had.

By preserving his memory, Cailloux's story continues to inspire future generations to advocate for justice and equality. He stands as a reminder that individual action can spark positive change and that courage and perseverance can prevail even in the face of seemingly insurmountable challenges.

## Lessons for Today: Relevance in Contemporary Struggles

André Cailloux's experiences deeply resonate with ongoing racial justice and social equality struggles. His fight against enslavement mirrors the ongoing battles against systemic racism and discrimination. His commitment to education remains a potent reminder of the importance of knowledge and empowerment in dismantling these systems.

Cailloux's leadership in the 1st Louisiana Native Guard challenges contemporary narratives about the role of African Americans in shaping the nation's history. It is a powerful counterpoint to the erasure of Black contributions and reminds you that the fight for freedom and equality has always been a collective effort.

By reflecting on Cailloux's journey, you'll gain a deeper understanding of the challenges and triumphs on the path toward a truly just and equitable society. His story urges you to confront the injustices that persist and challenge the systems perpetuating inequality. Continue the fight for a future where the ideals of equality and freedom truly flourish.

## André Cailloux: An Unforgettable Hero

André Cailloux's journey compels you to embrace education as a weapon against ignorance, service as a pathway toward collective progress, and resilience as the shield that protects you from despair. By holding the values embodied by André Cailloux close, you'll continue to honor his legacy and apply its lessons to your own life.

Let his spirit be your guiding light, his dedication your compass, and his resilience the shield that protects your resolve. By doing so, you'll honor his memory through words of admiration and by carrying the torch of his legacy forward, ensuring that his story continues to inspire generations to come.

In the end, André Cailloux's legacy is not defined by the battles he fought or the medals he earned but by his enduring impact on the world. He was an ordinary man who rose to the occasion, becoming a hero who fought for freedom and equality. In doing so, he immortalized his name in American history. Remember that even the smallest spark of courage ignites a flame that illuminates the path toward a brighter future.

# Chapter 9: Lydia Bixby: The Woman Behind the Lincoln Letter

As the storm clouds of the Civil War gathered, casting long shadows across the land, Lydia Bixby became an unwitting symbol of the war's agonizing human cost. This chapter explores her life in Boston, chronicling the momentous decision of her five sons to join the Union cause and the subsequent tragedy that unfolded. You'll witness her support for their cause and the crushing weight of each loss. Ultimately, you'll hear the poignant echo of President Lincoln's "Bixby Letter," a tribute to her immeasurable sacrifice and that of the countless mothers who bore the brunt of a nation's conflict.

LETTER FROM PRESIDENT LINCOLN. Mrs. Bixby —a lady in the southern portion of this city, whose case has excited much sympathy—had six sons enlisted in the Union army, five of whom have been killed in battle, and the sixth is now at the U.S. Hospital at Readville. Being in indigent circumstances, she has received asistance from some of the churches and Christian women of Boston. Her lonely abode was made cheerful this morning by the receipt of the following letter from President Lincoln:

EXECUTIVE MANSION,
WASHINGTON, Nov. 21, 1864.

*Dear Madam,*—I have been shown in the files of the War Department a statement of the Adjutant General of Massachusetts, that you are the mother of five sons who have died gloriously on the field of battle.

I feel how weak and fruitless must be any words of mine which should attempt to beguile you from the grief of a loss so overwhelming. But I cannot refrain from tendering to you the consolation that may be found in the thanks of the Republic they died to save.

I pray that our Heavenly Father may assuage the anguish of your bereavement, and leave you only the cherished memory of the loved and lost, and the solemn pride that must be yours, to have laid so costly a sacrifice upon the altar of Freedom.

Yours, very sincerely and respectfully,
MRS. BIXBY.                    A. LINCOLN.

President Lincoln's "Bixby Letter" was a tribute to Lydia Bixby's immeasurable sacrifice.

https://commons.wikimedia.org/wiki/File:Bixby_Letter_newspaper.jpg

# Life in Boston: The Calm Before the Storm

As the year 1861 dawned on Boston, a quiet calm settled over the city. It was the world Lydia Bixby knew, a familiar landscape of bustling streets, towering churches, and the salty tang of the nearby harbor. She had raised her family of five sons and three daughters in this haven, navigating the joys and challenges of life in a rapidly changing world.

Lydia's life was a woman of resilience and resourcefulness. As a widow, she had assumed the role of both father and mother, providing for her children and instilling a deep sense of duty and honor in them. Her sons were her pride and joy. These strong, hard-working young men carried the hopes and dreams of their families on their shoulders.

The societal landscape of pre-war Boston was a complex one. The winds of change were blowing, carrying with them whispers of abolitionist sentiments and growing tension between the North and South. Like many others, Lydia held onto a fragile hope that the brewing conflict could be resolved peacefully.

Yet, as the summer of 1861 arrived, the storm clouds of war gathered momentum. President Lincoln's call for troops reverberated across the nation, sparking a wave of patriotism and a sense of duty among young men across the land. The call resonated deeply with Lydia's sons.

# The Enlistment of Five Sons: Answering the Nation's Call

The decision to enlist was not taken lightly. Each son had dreams and aspirations, hopes for the future that intertwined with their love for their country and the ideals of freedom and liberty. The eldest, Charles, was a skilled shoemaker, his hands calloused from years of hard work. Oliver, the second eldest, was described as a "handsome youth" full of life and laughter. The younger sons, Henry, George, and Theodore, were still teenagers, their eyes filled with a mixture of excitement and apprehension.

The day of their departure was a bittersweet one. Pride swelled in Lydia's heart as she watched her sons march off, their faces resolute and their uniforms crisp and new. Yet, a gnawing fear tugged at her soul. The grim realities of war were not lost on her, and the potential for loss loomed large.

Despite her anxieties, Lydia remained steadfast. She knew that her sons were fighting for a cause greater than themselves and that their sacrifice could pave the way for a brighter future. She bade them farewell with a brave smile, her maternal strength a beacon of support even in the face of uncertainty.

As the months passed, news from the battlefields trickled in, each piece of information carrying the weight of life and death. Lydia followed the news with a heavy heart, her faith a fragile shield against the storm that raged around her.

The calm of Lydia's pre-war life had been shattered. The sons she had raised with love and care were now thrust into the heart of a brutal conflict, but in the middle of the uncertainty and fear, one thing remained constant. That was Lydia's undying love for her sons and the belief in the cause they were fighting for.

The storm clouds of war had descended on Lydia's world, and the calm before the storm had given way to a turbulent sea of uncertainty. As she faced the unknown future with courage, she was certain that the legacy of the Bixby boys would be etched in history. It was proof of the enduring power of family, love, and the brave pursuit of a just cause.

# Tragic Losses: Grief, Uncertainty, and the Toll of War

The storm that engulfed Lydia Bixby's world with the outbreak of the Civil War soon began to exact its devastating toll. One by one, news arrived of her sons' fates, each piece of information a searing blow that shattered the fragile hope she clung to.

### The Toll of War: Sons in Battle

Charles, the eldest, fell first, succumbing to wounds sustained at the Battle of Fredericksburg in December 1862. The news was like a physical blow to Lydia. The air suddenly sucked from her lungs as she grappled with the reality of her loss. Her eldest son, her pillar of strength, was gone.

Oliver, the second eldest, met a similar fate at the Battle of Antietam in September 1862. His death, just months after Charles, plunged Lydia deeper into the abyss of grief. The dreams she had once harbored for her sons, the hopes for their future, lay shattered at her feet.

Oliver, the second eldest son, passed away at the Battle of Antietam.
https://commons.wikimedia.org/wiki/File:Thure_de_Thulstrup_-_Battle_of_Antietam.jpg

Henry, captured at the Battle of Gettysburg in July 1863, disappeared into the labyrinthine prison system of the Confederacy. Months passed with no word, leaving Lydia's heart suspended in a state of agonizing uncertainty. Was he alive? Was he dead? The unknown gnawed at her, a constant companion in her solitude.

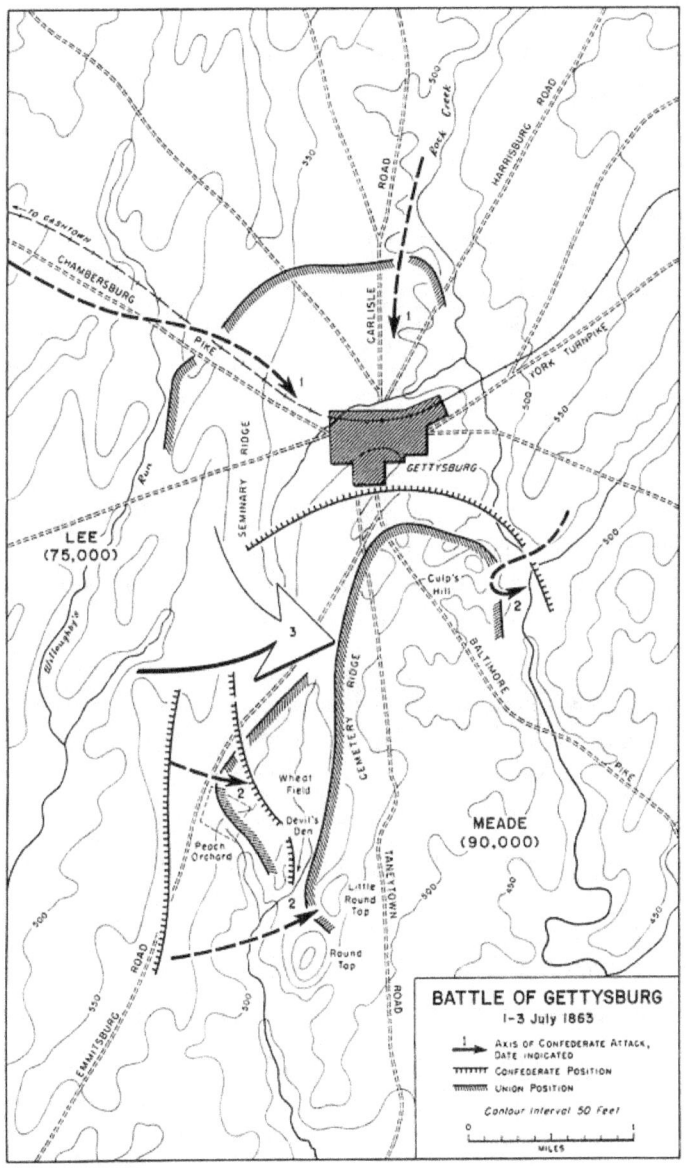

Map of the Battle of Gettyburg.
https://commons.wikimedia.org/wiki/File:Battle_of_Gettysburg_map.jpg

George, captured at the Battle of Chickamauga in September 1863, followed his brother into the dark depths of Confederate prison camps. Lydia's hopes of seeing her sons again dwindled with each passing day. Grief, once a sharp pain, now settled into a dull ache that permeated her every waking moment. Though his true fate was unknown, his absence was counted as a grievous loss, as well.

Theodore, the youngest, faced a different fate. He went missing during a skirmish near Petersburg, Virginia, in June 1864. Whether he was captured, killed, or simply deserted, no one knew. The uncertainty surrounding his fate became another constant torment for Lydia, a wound that refused to heal.

### Grieving Mother: A Nation in Mourning

Lydia Bixby's grief was profound and personal. She was a mother who had lost not one but possibly five sons. The backbone of her family, her source of pride and joy, were all gone. She mourned each loss in the quiet confines of her home, tears soaking her pillow and prayers escaping her lips.

Her grief was not hers alone. It mirrored the collective sorrow of a nation grappling with the carnage of war. Thousands of mothers across the land shared her anguish, their hearts heavy with the weight of loss. Lydia's story resonated with a nation in mourning, her tragedy becoming a symbol of the immense cost of war.

President Lincoln, touched by Lydia's plight, penned a letter expressing his condolences. His words, while offering solace, could not mend her shattered heart. The nation mourned with her, recognizing in her grief the reflection of their collective loss.

As the war finally drew to a close, Lydia emerged from the depths of grief a changed woman. Though forever marked by her losses, she found strength in the memory of her sons and the unwavering support of her community. Her tragedy became a reminder of the human cost of war and the sacrifices made for the ideals of freedom and equality.

### Abraham Lincoln's Bixby Letter: Symbolism Amidst Sorrows

In the Civil War's devastation, a poignant gesture offered a glimmer of solace and empathy to a grieving mother. President Abraham Lincoln's letter to Lydia Bixby, written in November 1864, transcends the medium to become a powerful symbol of a nation mourning its fallen sons.

### The Famed Bixby Letter: A Presidential Consolation

The letter, composed in Lincoln's characteristically eloquent style, expresses heartfelt condolences to Lydia Bixby. Lincoln acknowledges the devastating impact of her loss, writing, *"I pray that our Heavenly Father may assuage the anguish of your bereavement, and leave you only the cherished memory of the loved and lost, and the solemn pride that must be yours to have laid so costly a sacrifice upon the altar of freedom."*

The mere fact that the President of the United States took the time to personally console a bereaved mother in the middle of a national crisis was a very powerful gesture. It demonstrated Lincoln's deep understanding of the human cost of war and his genuine compassion for those suffering its consequences.

Beyond offering comfort, the letter also acknowledged the immense sacrifices made by families like the Bixbys. By recognizing Lydia's sons as "a costly sacrifice upon the altar of freedom," Lincoln elevated their losses to the level of national significance.

### Debates on Authenticity: Unraveling the Letter's Mysteries

Over the years, the Bixby letter has been shrouded in controversy and debate. Some have questioned its authenticity, suggesting that it was penned by one of Lincoln's secretaries rather than the President himself. Others have argued that Lydia Bixby may not have even lost five sons in the war, further fueling doubts surrounding the context of the letter.

While the authorial question remains unresolved, historians acknowledge the letter's significance as a powerful symbolic gesture, regardless of its origins. Whether written by Lincoln himself or one of his trusted advisors, the letter effectively captured the spirit of the era and the nation's grief over its wartime losses.

# Symbolic Significance: A Nation's Gratitude and Empathy

The Bixby letter transcended its recipient to become a symbol of the collective grief and gratitude felt by the nation. As news of the letter spread, Lydia Bixby became an unwitting representative of all mothers who had lost children in the war.

The letter was a public acknowledgment of the immense sacrifices made by families on the home front. It offered a sense of unity and shared sorrow, reminding the nation that the war's impact extended far beyond the battlefields.

The letter resonated with the broader themes of sacrifice and redemption that were central to the Civil War narrative. By honoring the memory of fallen soldiers and offering solace to their families, the letter solidified the war's purpose and the sacrifices made in the pursuit of freedom.

# Lydia Bixby: A Poignant Figure in Civil War History

During the Civil War, countless families grappled with unimaginable sacrifice. Among them, Lydia Bixby's story encapsulates the profound personal costs borne by so many during that turbulent era. Her experience transcends the realm of individual tragedy, transforming her into a symbolic representation of the countless mothers who faced similar heartaches and stoically persevered.

### Beyond Personal Tragedy: A Mother Symbolizing Many

Lydia's story is not unique. Thousands of mothers across the divided nation faced similar losses, their lives forever altered by the war's insatiable appetite for young lives. Yet, it is in the universality of her experience that Lydia's significance lies. She was a symbol for all those mothers who endured unimaginable loss with quiet dignity and unwavering strength.

Her story is a stark reminder of the human cost of war, a cost often measured not in grand battles or strategic victories but in the shattered lives of families left behind. Through Lydia, you see the deeply personal impact of conflict, the invisible scars etched onto the souls of those who have suffered its devastating consequences.

### Historical Memory: Lydia Bixby's Enduring Impact

The story of Lydia Bixby would likely have faded into the obscurity of history had it not been for a single act of profound empathy. President Lincoln's letter ensured that Lydia Bixby's story would not be forgotten. It captured the nation's attention, prompting a wave of public sympathy and support for her and other families who had lost loved ones in the war. Her story found its way into newspapers, books, and historical accounts, becoming a permanent fixture in the collective memory of the Civil War.

More importantly, her story was a powerful tool for reflection. It invited Americans to confront the true costs of the war and to consider the human cost beyond the battlefield victories. Her story sparked conversations about the responsibility of leadership, the importance of empathy, and the need to honor the sacrifices of those who had served.

Today, Lydia Bixby's legacy continues to inspire. Her name appears on memorials and tributes dedicated to those who lost loved ones in the Civil War. Her story is taught in classrooms, ensuring that future generations will remember the sacrifices made by ordinary people during extraordinary times.

### Lydia Bixby's Enduring Legacy

The ink on President Lincoln's letter had barely dried before Lydia Bixby's story began its remarkable journey into the collective American memory. Her name became synonymous with the sacrifices endured by countless families during the Civil War.

### Commemorations and Memorials: Preserving Lydia Bixby's Memory

In the small Boston neighborhood where she lived, a simple plaque on the brick wall of a church commemorates Lydia's life. The inscription reads, "Lydia Bixby, a Mother of the Civil War." This modest tribute stands in stark contrast to the grandeur of the national monuments erected in honor of war heroes. Yet, its simplicity speaks volumes, reminding visitors of the quiet tragedies that often unfold behind the larger narrative of war.

Beyond this local tribute, Lydia's story has found its way into museums, historical archives, and classrooms across the nation. Her image adorns textbooks, her name etched onto veterans' memorials. In 2017, a portrait of her was unveiled at the National Portrait Gallery in Washington, D.C., solidifying her place among the nation's most recognized historical figures. These tangible commemorations ensure that Lydia's story is not forgotten. They remind you of the human cost of war and the enduring strength of those who carry its burden.

### Lessons for Today: Relevance in Contemporary Struggles

Lydia Bixby's story resonates with profound relevance even today. As you witness families torn apart by conflicts around the world, you are reminded of the sacrifices made by mothers and loved ones. Her experience compels you to confront the unspoken truths of war, to acknowledge the pain and grief that ripple outward far beyond the battlefield.

Lydia's story also imparts empathy, particularly in the context of presidential leadership. President Lincoln's heartfelt letter to Lydia displays compassion in a time of immense suffering. It demonstrates the profound impact that leaders have through their words and actions, offering solace and recognition to those who have borne the brunt of conflict. In an age of political division and social discord, Lydia Bixby's story calls you to bridge divides and foster empathy. It invites you to recognize the shared humanity that binds people together, regardless of differences.

As you reflect on Lydia Bixby, remember the vast multitude of mothers, fathers, daughters, sons, and families whose lives are forever altered by war. Let their stories inspire you to strive for a more peaceful world. Lydia Bixby's legacy endures not only in the memorials erected in her honor but also in the hearts and minds of those who encounter her story.

# Chapter 10: Thomas Nast: Art and War

In the landscape of the Civil War, battles raged with the clash of steel and thunderous cannons. Here, Thomas Nast emerged as a formidable force, wielding a weapon far more powerful than any soldier's musket. His weapon of choice? His pen. Through his incisive and often scathing political cartoons, Nast carved a path through the complexities of the era. He shaped public opinion and ideologies with each stroke. This chapter uncovers the extraordinary journey of this German immigrant, who transformed from a young apprentice to a political cartoonist.

**Thomas Nast was a formidable force.**
*Thomas Nast, CC0, via Wikimedia Commons:*
*https://commons.wikimedia.org/wiki/File:Portrait_of_Thomas_Nast_MET_DP860194.jpg*

# Origins: A Sketch of Early Life and Artistic Initiation

From the cobblestone streets of Landau, Germany, to the bustling avenues of New York City, the life of Thomas Nast unfolded in a series of dramatic strokes. Each phase of his life contributed to his profound impact on American history as a political cartoonist. His early life and artistic initiation laid the groundwork for his remarkable career, shaping the vision and voice that would later satirize and redefine the political landscape of the United States.

### A Journey from Germany to America: The Making of an Illustrator

Born in 1840, Nast's childhood in Germany was marked by the tumultuous political climate of the Vormärz period. The revolutionary fervor of the time undoubtedly shaped his young mind, fostering a keen awareness of social injustice and political manipulation. In 1846, at the tender age of six, Nast journeyed across the Atlantic with his parents, seeking a new life in the burgeoning American republic.

Their arrival in New York City marked a turning point for young Nast. The vibrant city, pulsating with energy and opportunity, provided the perfect backdrop for his artistic talent to flourish. While the circumstances of their immigration remain relatively unknown, it is believed that financial hardship forced Nast to leave school at a young age. However, this setback did not dampen his artistic spirit. Instead, it ignited a passion for illustration, a medium that would become his powerful tool for social commentary and political satire.

### Illustration: Early Steps in a New World

With an unwavering determination and a natural talent for drawing, Nast began his artistic journey by apprenticing at Frank Leslie's Illustrated Newspaper. This publishing house was a fertile ground for him to hone his skills and develop his unique style. He diligently learned the craft of wood engraving, a laborious process that demanded precision and attention to detail.

While at Frank Leslie's, Nast encountered both challenges and opportunities. He faced fierce competition from established illustrators and had to navigate the demands of a fast-paced publishing environment. However, he also found mentors and collaborators who recognized his potential and helped him refine his artistic voice.

One of his early collaborations was with Theodore Roosevelt Sr., a prominent businessman and philanthropist. Together, they created a series of illustrations for "Harper's Weekly," a magazine with a national audience. This collaboration proved to be a turning point in Nast's career, providing him with a platform to showcase his talents and reach a wider audience.

As his reputation grew, Nast began to receive commissions from other major publications. He honed his skills in capturing expressions, creating caricatured figures, and utilizing symbolism to convey complex political messages. His early works tackled various social and political issues, including corruption, Tammany Hall politics, and the plight of the working class.

Through his early work, Nast established himself as a rising star in the field of illustration. His keen eye for detail, his wit, and his ability to translate complex ideas into powerful visual narratives quickly garnered him a loyal following. These early years were crucial in shaping his artistic identity and laying the foundation for his later contributions to American political discourse.

Nast's early life and artistic initiation were marked by both hardship and opportunity. His journey from a young immigrant in New York City to a respected illustrator laid the groundwork for his impactful career as a political cartoonist. The lessons learned, the challenges overcome, and the skills honed during this formative period would later serve him well as he became one of the most influential figures in American history.

### Harper's Weekly: Nast's Artistic Arsenal in the Civil War

The pages of "Harper's Weekly" were Thomas Nast's artistic arsenal during the American Civil War. With his potent illustrations, he documented the conflict and actively shaped public opinion, influencing the course of history. It's time to explore Nast's collaboration with "Harper's Weekly," highlighting the impact of his work on the nation's understanding of the war and its key figures.

### Joining "Harper's Weekly": Nast's Artistic Platform

In 1859, Nast landed a position as an illustrator at "Harper's Weekly," a leading publication in the United States. This platform provided him with an unparalleled opportunity to reach a wide audience, estimated to be over 200,000 readers at its peak. The editorial environment at "Harper's Weekly" was fervent and politically charged. It fostered Nast's burgeoning talent and encouraged him to use his art as a tool for social commentary.

Within this dynamic environment, Nast's artistic voice found its niche. He developed a unique style that combined caricature with realistic detail, creating powerful visual narratives that captured the essence of the times. His keen eye for observation and his ability to convey complex emotions through his illustrations quickly made him a popular figure among readers.

## Battlefield Realities: Illustrating the Visceral Truths of War

The outbreak of the Civil War in 1861 presented Nast with a new artistic challenge. He was tasked with depicting the brutal realities of the battlefield for an audience eager for news from the front lines. With his illustrations, he brought the war home, capturing the horrors and heroism witnessed on the battlefield.

His artwork often featured graphic depictions of wounded soldiers, destroyed landscapes, and the grim aftermath of battles. This unflinching portrayal of war's true costs was a stark counterpoint to the romanticized narratives often presented in other media outlets. Nast's illustrations played a crucial role in informing the public about the war's true nature, shattering illusions and inspiring introspection.

## Demonizing the Confederacy: Nast's Artistic Allegiance

Nast's artistry became a potent weapon in the fight against the Confederacy. He used his pen to demonize the Southern cause, portraying Confederate leaders as cruel, greedy, and uncivilized. This visual representation contributed significantly to the North's war effort by solidifying public opinion against the Confederacy and generating support for the Union cause.

**THE PAST AND THE FUTURE.**

Nast's artistry became a potent weapon in the fight against the Confederacy.

*Thomas Nast, CC BY-SA 4.0 <https://creativecommons.org/licenses/by-sa/4.0>, via Wikimedia Commons: https://commons.wikimedia.org/wiki/File:Library_Company_of_Philadelphia_1865-3_variant_101540.F_Thomas_Nast_Emancipation_crop_and_straighten_and_brighten_from_tiff.jpg*

One of his most iconic illustrations from this period is "Compromise with the South," published in 1864. This powerful image depicts a monstrous figure representing the Confederacy devouring the Constitution, symbolizing its threat to the very foundation of American democracy. Such illustrations resonated deeply with northern audiences, further solidifying their resolve to fight for the Union.

# Support for President Lincoln: The Pen as Political Endorsement

Nast's unwavering support for President Lincoln was evident throughout the war. He used his illustrations to champion Lincoln's policies, portraying him as a strong and resolute leader in times of crisis. His depiction of Lincoln as the "Great Emancipator" played a crucial role in shaping public perception of the president and his commitment to ending slavery.

One of the most iconic images of Lincoln created by Nast is "Uncle Sam's Proclamation," published in 1862. This illustration features a stern and determined Uncle Sam pointing towards the Emancipation Proclamation, symbolizing the president's commitment to ending slavery. Illustrations like that were powerful endorsements of Lincoln's leadership and contributed to his re-election in 1864.

### The "Emancipation" Series: Championing Abolitionist Sentiments

In American history, very few artists have wielded their talents with such impactful fervor as Thomas Nast. During the Civil War, Nast's artistic arsenal extended beyond mere illustration. It became a powerful weapon in the fight against slavery. At the heart of his legacy stands the "Emancipation" series, a collection of artwork calling for abolition and a powerful visual narrative of freedom's dawn.

### The "Emancipation" Series: Art as Advocacy

The "Emancipation" series perfectly portrays Nast's artistic prowess and his commitment to abolition. Composed of several distinct illustrations, each piece meticulously crafted a visual tapestry that spoke volumes about the dehumanization of slavery and the yearning for freedom.

One of the most striking pieces in the series is "The Slave Auction." This harrowing illustration depicts a young woman being auctioned off, her gaze filled with despair and resignation. The stark contrast between the callous indifference of the auctioneer and the woman's suffering is a powerful indictment of the barbarity of slavery.

Beyond capturing the immediate horrors of the auction block, Nast's series also looked towards the future. In "The Past, Present, and Future of the Negro Race," he envisioned a future where slavery was abolished and African Americans were free to pursue education, employment, and self-determination. This powerful vision provided hope for abolitionists, reinforcing their conviction that freedom was not only attainable but imperative.

### Impact on Abolitionist Sentiments: Shaping Public Opinion

The "Emancipation" series resonated deeply with the American public, playing a crucial role in shaping public opinion on the issue of slavery. Published in "Harper's Weekly," a widely circulated magazine with a readership exceeding 200,000, Nast's illustrations reached a broad audience and sparked conversations in homes and communities across the nation.

His artwork exposed the brutality of the institution and humanized the enslaved. The sketches portrayed them as individuals with hopes, dreams, and families. This humanizing touch resonated with readers, fostering empathy and understanding for the plight of enslaved individuals and furthering support for the abolitionist cause.

Nast's series provided a powerful counterpoint to the romanticized narratives of slavery often presented in other forms of media. By depicting the harsh realities of life under bondage, he challenged the prevailing perceptions and forced Americans to confront the moral implications of slavery.

The influence of the "Emancipation" series extended beyond public opinion. It was a vital tool for abolitionist organizations, who utilized the illustrations as educational materials and fundraising tools. These powerful images solidified the abolitionist movement and galvanized support for the Union cause, ultimately contributing to the end of slavery in the United States.

# Post-War Illustrations: Advocacy for Justice and Equality

The guns of the Civil War may have fallen silent, but Thomas Nast's artistic voice continued to resonate, urging the nation toward a more just and equitable future. His post-war illustrations reveal an artist undeterred by the cessation of hostilities, relentlessly wielding his pen to advocate for the rights of the disenfranchised and champion the cause of a truly unified America.

### Continuing the Fight: Nast's Post-War Artistic Activism

The years following the war saw Nast turn his artistic focus to the challenges of Reconstruction. He exposed the injustices faced by newly freed African Americans who were denied basic rights and subjected to violence and discrimination. His illustrations frequently depicted the Ku Klux Klan, a notorious White supremacist organization, as menacing figures, shedding light on their terror tactics and the plight of their victims.

One such illustration is "The Ku Klux Klan: A Warning to the South," published in 1871. This powerful image features Klansmen clad in White robes and hoods, menacing a Black family in their home. Nast's use of stark contrast and dramatic lighting amplifies the scene's horror. It's a stark indictment of the Klan's violence and a call for action to protect the rights of African Americans.

Beyond exposing racial injustices, Nast also addressed the issue of political corruption. He attacked the Tammany Hall political machine in New York City, portraying its members as greedy and corrupt figures who exploited the city's resources for personal gain. His cartoons, such as "The Tammany Tiger Loose," played a significant role in raising public awareness and ultimately contributed to the downfall of the corrupt organization.

### Impact on Post-War Reconstruction: A Visual Commentary

Nast's post-war illustrations were a vital visual commentary on the complexities of Reconstruction. They captured the hopes and aspirations of newly freed African Americans for a better future while simultaneously exposing the forces that sought to deny them their rightful place in society.

His artwork provided a platform for marginalized voices and challenged the dominant narratives of the time. He used his illustrations to educate the public, spark debate, and ultimately promote social change. In doing so, he played a crucial role in shaping the post-war landscape and laying the groundwork for the ongoing struggle for racial justice and equality.

Despite the immense impact of his work, Nast faced significant opposition. His relentless criticism of powerful figures and institutions often generated controversy and even threats. However, he remained undeterred, unwavering in his commitment to using his artistic talents to advocate for a fairer and more just society.

### The Pen as a Mighty Sword: Nast's Heroism in Art

While history remembers heroes of the battlefield, Thomas Nast's heroism unfolded on a different canvas. His weapon was a pen. His battlefield was the vast expanse of American public opinion. With his powerful illustrations, Nast had an influence that transcended the limitations of physical might, etching his name in the annals of American history as a champion of justice and an architect of social change.

# Nast's Heroism Defined: Art as a Catalyst for Change

Unlike the soldiers who faced cannons and bullets, Nast confronted the entrenched forces of prejudice, corruption, and injustice with his ink. He exposed the horrors of slavery, ignited the flames of abolitionism, and held powerful figures accountable through the scathing satire and biting wit of his art. His illustrations were weapons forged in the crucible of conviction, aimed at the hearts and minds of a nation grappling with its identity.

Nast's heroism resided in his unwavering commitment to using his talents for the betterment of society. He possessed the courage to challenge the status quo, to speak truth to power, and to give voice to the marginalized and oppressed. His illustrations were not just reflections of reality. They were catalysts for change, igniting public discourse, shaping political agendas, and ultimately influencing the course of history.

### Legacy of Influence: Nast's Enduring Impact

Beyond the immediate impact of his work, Nast's legacy continues to inspire artists and activists to use their talents for social change. His influence is evident in the works of contemporary artists who address issues of social injustice, political corruption, and inequality.

Nast's cartoons remain relevant even today, accentuating the power of art to spark dialogue, challenge authority, and inspire action. His legacy teaches you that the pen can be as powerful as the sword. Art can be a tool for social progress, and individual voices, when amplified through creativity and conviction, can change the course of history.

By wielding his pen with courage and conviction, Thomas Nast transcended the limitations of his time and medium. He became a hero not through physical prowess but through the transformative power of his art. He left behind a legacy that continues to inspire and challenge people to this day. His story reminds you that true heroes are often not found on the battlefield but on the canvas of human creativity, where the ink of conviction writes the future.

# Conclusion

As you conclude your exploration of the lives and contributions of individuals like Elijah P. Marrs, Susie King Taylor, and Thomas Nast, you might feel a profound sense of admiration for their courage, sacrifice, and resilience. Their stories, etched against the backdrop of the American Civil War, transcend the battlefield and resonate with timeless themes of heroism.

### Beyond the Battlefield: Diverse Forms of Bravery

These individuals, each unique in their backgrounds and motivations, embody diverse forms of bravery that defy conventional definitions. You witness Marrs' unwavering fight for self-liberation, Edmonds' daring deception in service of the Union cause, Carney's valiant defense of the flag amidst the chaos of battle, and Bixby's quiet strength as a symbol of the war's profound human cost. Their narratives intermingle to form a powerful tapestry of heroism that transcends the limitations of a single battlefield.

### Contemporary Relevance

The legacies of these heroes offer a potent lens through which to examine contemporary challenges. Their unwavering commitment to justice, unity, and perseverance provides a roadmap for navigating the complexities of the modern world. As you grapple with issues of social inequality, political polarization, and the enduring quest for equality, the lessons gleaned from their lives serve as a guiding light.

## A Call to Action: Building a More Equitable Future

In a world often characterized by division and apathy, their stories remind you of the collective power people possess to effect positive change. Their unwavering resolve inspires all to challenge the status quo, champion the marginalized, and strive toward a more equitable future. Their legacies are not mere historical anecdotes. They are a call to action, urging you to embrace the values they so valiantly upheld.

### Key Takeaways

- **Diverse Forms of Heroism:** The Civil War heroes showcase the multifaceted nature of courage, extending beyond the traditional battlefield soldier.
- **Enduring Relevance:** The values of justice, unity, and perseverance championed by these heroes remain crucial in tackling contemporary challenges.
- **Collective Power for Change:** Their stories inspire you to harness the power of individual actions to create a more just and equitable society.
- **Continuous Inspiration:** The legacies of these heroes are a timeless reminder of the potential for human courage and resilience.

### Echoes of the Past, Shaping the Future

The American Civil War may be a distant chapter in history, but the echoes of its heroes' deeds still reverberate through time. By learning from their sacrifices, embracing their values, and channeling their spirit of resilience, you will build a future where the ideals they fought for (freedom, equality, and justice) are not mere aspirations but the very foundation of society.

# Check out another book in the series

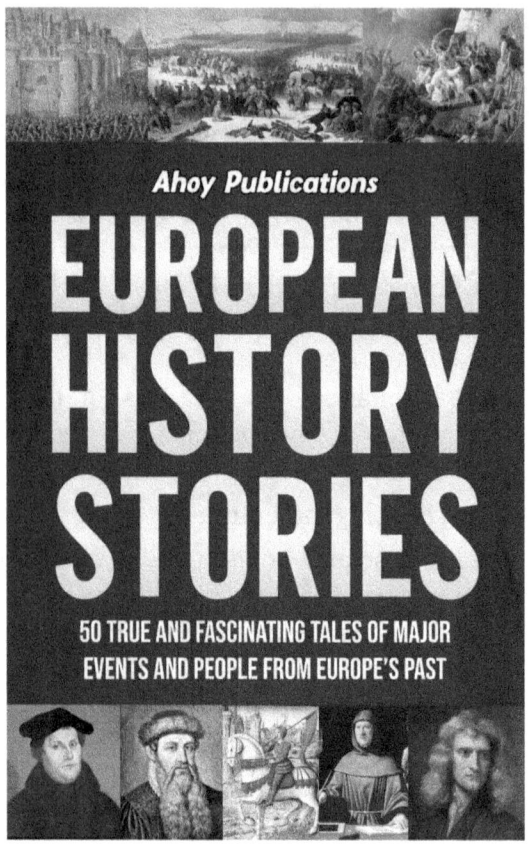

# References

Abraham Lincoln Online. (n.d.). Letter to Mrs. Bixby. Www.abrahamlincolnonline.org. https://www.abrahamlincolnonline.org/lincoln/speeches/bixby.htm

American Battlefield Trust. (2019a, February 26). Albert Cashier, aka Jennie Hodgers. Battlefields. https://www.battlefields.org/learn/biographies/albert-cashier

American Battlefield Trust. (2019b, April 10). Susie Taylor. American Battlefield Trust. https://www.battlefields.org/learn/biographies/susie-taylor

Chiles, K., & Kirby, H. (2023, March 23). Martin R. Delany. Oxford Bibliographies. https://www.oxfordbibliographies.com/abstract/document/obo-9780190280024/obo-9780190280024-0117.xml

Mitchell, B. (2023, May 26). Andre Cailloux: First Black Officer to Die in the Civil War. Abraham Lincoln Presidential Library and Museum. https://presidentlincoln.illinois.gov/Blog/Posts/177/African-American-History/2023/5/Andre-Cailloux-The-Hero-of-Port-Hudson/blog-post/

Morawski, L. A., & Smith, N. (2000). Elijah P. Marrs, b. 1840. Life and History of the Rev. Elijah P. Marrs, First Pastor of Beargrass Baptist Church, and Author. Documenting the American South. https://docsouth.unc.edu/neh/marrs/marrs.html

National Park Service. (2017, September 14). Sarah Emma Edmonds (U.S. National Park Service). National Park Service. https://www.nps.gov/people/sarah-emma-edmonds.htm

Page, J. (n.d.). William H. Carney (U.S. National Park Service). National Park Service. https://www.nps.gov/articles/william-h-carney.htm

Shelby, T. (2003). Two Conceptions of Black Nationalism: Martin Delany on the Meaning of Black Political Solidarity. Political Theory, 31(5), 664–692. http://www.jstor.org/stable/3595691